D0781867

Wolf That I Am

Saginaw Chippewa Tribal College
2274 Enterprise Drive
Mt. Pleasant, MI 48858

Wolf That I Am

In Search of the Red Earth People

— ◇ —

FRED McTAGGART

Foreword by William T. Hagan

University of Oklahoma Press : Norman

Library of Congress Cataloging-in-Publication Data

McTaggart, Fred.
  Wolf that I am.

  Reprint. Originally published: Boston : Houghton Mifflin, 1976.
With new foreword by W. T. Hagan.
  Bibliography: p. 193.
  Includes index.
  1. Fox Indians. 2. McTaggart, Fred. 3. Fox Indians—Legends. 4. Indians of North America—Iowa—Legends.
I. Title.
E99.F7M32   1984   977.7'00497   84-7352
ISBN 0-8061-1905-5 (pbk.)

Copyright © 1976 by Fred McTaggart except for the foreword, by William T. Hagan, copyright © 1984 by the University of Oklahoma Press, Norman, Publishing Division of the University. Manufactured in the U.S.A. First printing of the paperback edition, 1984.

2   3   4   5   6   7   8   9   10

For Donna
and for Duncan and Brendan
—the Center of My Universe

Contents

	Page	
Foreword by William T. Hagan		ix
Preface to the Paperback Edition		xv
Acknowledgments		xvii
Chapter 1		1
2		4
3		8
4		20
5		30
6		34
7		41
8		50
9		54
10		56
11		60
12		65
13		67
14		72
15		78
16		82
17		91
18		97
19		101
20		105
21		109
22		116
23		123
24		129
25		135

Chapter 26   141
        27   149
        28   154
        29   156
        30   162
        31   167
        32   174
        33   180
        34   185
Guide to Further Reading   193
Index   197

Foreword

by William T. Hagan

In the spring of 1974, while visiting the Center for the History of the American Indian at the Newberry Library, I conferred with the Center fellows who were in residence. My role was to discuss with them their research projects and, hopefully, to give them some advice and counsel. One of the fellows that spring was Fred McTaggart, who, I was told, was doing something on the Iowa Foxes. As I was the author of a history of the Sac and Fox Indians, this promised to be one occasion when perhaps I really could be of some help. My recollection after a period of ten years, however, is that this was not one of the sessions from which I emerged believing that I had made a contribution.

McTaggart and I seemed to be operating on different wavelengths. I was anxious to help, but he, while pleasant, seemed somewhat reserved and not anxious to tap my knowledge, however limited, of Iowa Fox history. This became more understandable when I learned that his discipline was English, not history, and that his original objective had been to collect Fox stories. Nevertheless, there was something about his manner that discouraged me from pressing him for details about his own research. When I read this book, I began to understand better what had happened. His memory of his first difficult meeting with the Foxes, when he was met with courteous reserve, reminded me of my encounter with McTaggart. Just as his cultural background had not prepared him for what he found among the Foxes, someone of my generation and professional training would require more than a few minutes to establish intellectual rapport with someone from another discipline who was as sensitive and so much of his own generation as Fred McTaggart.

The task that McTaggart had set for himself, to know the Foxes, was an ambitious one. In one sense it was relatively easy, because of extensive work done among them in the 1940s and 1950s by the University of Chicago anthropologists headed by Professor Sol Tax. The Iowa Foxes had been a laboratory for a Tax innovation, "action anthropology," which has been described by one of its practitioners, Frederick O. Gearing, as helping while learning and learning while help-ing. For several years a succession of anthropology students resided among the Foxes, and their work made that small community one of the most thoroughly studied of all Native American groups.

Unfortunately for McTaggart, by the late 1960s the Iowa Foxes had concluded, justifiably or not, that some of the information gleaned by the University of Chicago students and other scholars had been used against them. This had made the Foxes even more difficult to approach, and as a people determined to preserve their cultural heritage, they had never been easy to interview. Certainly the history of their relations with the whites could have made them wary.

The people among whom Fred McTaggart ventured in 1973 have been known under a variety of names. That of Fox was applied to them by Frenchmen who failed to under-stand that an Indian being quizzed had named his clan, not his tribe. That happened in the seventeenth century. By the nineteenth century, because of their close relationship with the Sac Tribe, they had been lumped with them, as the Sac and Fox Indians, by American authorities. By the 1930s the official designation of the band of Foxes living in Iowa had become the Sac and Fox of the Mississippi in Iowa. Through-out that period their name for themselves was, as it is today, the Mesquakies, which can be translated as Red Earth People.

The Mesquakies, allied with the Sacs, supported the British in the Revolution. In 1804, when a delegation of Sacs visited Saint Louis to try to smooth over a recent frontier clash, they were prevailed on to agree to a treaty, by which the confederated Sacs and Foxes sold to the United States their claims to an area occupied by both tribes in northwestern Illinois and southwestern Wisconsin. It is highly unlikely that the members of the delegation totally comprehended what had transpired. Governor William Henry Harrison of Indiana Territory, who represented the United States, was notorious for his questionable tactics in many negotiations with tribes south of the Great Lakes.

The 1804 treaty contained a provision which became, in effect, a time bomb. The Sacs and Foxes were not required to remove immediately from the land to which the United States now held title. The treaty did require that they surrender the land when it became needed for white settlement. For twenty years the Sacs and Foxes were left in peaceful possession of the land that had been their home for generations, even after they sided with the British in the War of 1812 and defeated American forces sent against them. After the war the Sacs and Foxes were required to sign another treaty reaffirming their 1804 cession, and the United States erected a fort near the principal Sac and Fox villages. Nevertheless, it was unlikely that more than a handful of the tribesmen were aware that they were residing in the area on borrowed time.

Not until the summer of 1828 did pressure from the state of Illinois finally produce the first demand that the Sacs and Foxes abandon the land ceded by the 1804 treaty and take up new homes in Iowa. They did not go quietly. Only after four years of threats and alarms, culminating in the Black Hawk War of 1832, were all of the Sacs and Foxes finally forced to remove. Meanwhile, the United States had taken the resistance of those Sacs and Foxes led by Black Hawk as justification for extorting another cession from the

Indians, this time a portion of the land that they claimed along the west bank of the Mississippi.

In the ten years that elapsed after the Black Hawk War the Sac and Fox were coerced into agreeing to two more treaties, by which they sold their remaining land in Iowa. The second of the two treaties also provided that they would emigrate to a new reservation set aside for them in Kansas. Nor would those cessions end the pressures upon these Indians to cede land for white settlement. In 1867 the Sacs and Foxes would be prevailed upon to sign still another treaty, this time requiring them to move still farther south, to what would become Oklahoma.

Meanwhile, many of the Mesquakies, as they continued to call themselves, had never left Iowa, and some of those who had been escorted to Kansas under armed guard had managed to return. For several years the Indians clung to their foothold in Iowa, and periodically troops would be sent to round up any who could be caught and transport them to Kansas. Just as quickly the Mesquakies would slip away from the Kansas reservation and return to Iowa.

Then the Mesquakies got the break that they had been hoping for. The state of Iowa authorized the purchase of land by these Indians, and in 1857 they began to acquire what would become 3,500 acres on the Iowa River. In 1870, 300 Mesquakies were living on that land, and the number was growing.

It would take the Mesquakies longer to achieve a separate political identity. Not until 1896 would the federal government take over from the state of Iowa the trust responsibility for the Mesquakie land on Iowa River. Then the new relationship was not a harmonious one. Almost immediately the Indians were exposed to the government's not-always-subtle pressure for assimilation. To achieve that goal, the Bureau of Indian Affairs insisted that the Indian children attend school. For years the bone of contention was a boarding school to which the children were sent. The Mesquakies finally were able to get a day school opened on their reservation, and then the control of that school became a source of conflict.

When Fred McTaggart ventured among the Mesquakies, they had only recently resisted the closing of the day school and the transfer of the Indian children to an off-reservation school attended by white children. Under the circumstances it is little wonder that the Mesquakies failed to clasp to their bosoms another white man appearing among them to, as they saw it, penetrate their inner mysteries and expose them to the world.

What did happen over the course of a year was that some of them came to know and respect this gentle, perceptive young man, and he came to know something of the Mesquakies, and in the process, to learn more about himself. This is the human story Fred McTaggart tells so well.

William T. Hagan

Fredonia, New York

Preface to the Paperback Edition

I FEEL NOW more than ever that *Wolf That I Am* is a work that requires revision with each passing of the seasons. Even though I would change nothing in the book, I know much about the stories today that I did not know then. For the past ten years I have been far removed from Mesquakie stories and the land on which they grow, but their teachings continue to nourish me with fresh insights as the years and circumstances change my perspective.

The Mesquakies seem always to travel with a part of me. At a time a few years ago when I faced a serious personal crisis, I received almost mystically a letter from a man I did not know, a railroad brakeman who lives near the Mesquakie settlement. "Just thought you'd be interested in seeing this postcard of Jack Wolfskin's new painting of Red Earth People with Bundles in Fog in Illinios."

My sporadic contacts with the Mesquakies—a meeting at a symposium, a letter from Isabel Sturgeon and her daughter in Colorado, a postcard from James North, an occasional call from John Sturgeon—tell me that almost nothing has changed since my visits in 1973 and 1974, perhaps since the Chicago project of the 1950s. The factional dispute still wrenches at hearts; the issues surrounding the day school are always in sharp focus; middle-aged Mesquakies still fret that the younger generation will lose their culture. Mesquakies change as does the burr oak tree across from my house—imperceptibly yet profoundly.

Isabel Sturgeon, a member of the Wolf clan, says that the story of the Raccoon and the Wolf is used to teach children and others to orient themselves in relation to the river and to know and recognize trees. "It brings to my mind about the trees. I have heard that so many times. I could hear it yet. My children had heard them, but they want to hear more."

John Sturgeon, proud that he has now passed the age of fifty, points out that trees as well as animals are blessed with powers. A wickiup is always made with ironwood "because they last longer that way." And, I presume, one who pays no heed to the grandfather trees and their orientation to the water is not listening to stories with the discipline that is required.

The ancient ledger still exists in Henry Sturgeon's back room, but the woman whose role it is to update the genealogies is no longer doing it. "But why can't someone else keep it?" asks the naïve outsider, and the Mesquakies reply with silence.

Isabel Sturgeon says: "We have tried to get together with Charlie Laveur and was with him one evening with the children. His home was an ideal place to talk and tell stories. It was a sacred place and we would have to be very, very careful of what we do there."

In order to respect the privacy of those with whom I talked, I provided fictional names that attempted to conceal clan identity. "People have been guessing who those characters are in the book, and some have to be told who they are," says Isabel Sturgeon. Perhaps the fictional names were unnecessary; at least, I want to apologize to John Buffalo, an intense and dedicated young Mesquakie of the Fish clan I first met in 1983. He has no relation to the John Buffalo of my story.

Acknowledgments

THE INTERSTATE highway traveler, en route to the breathtaking beauty of the Rocky Mountains, often complains about the boring and endless drive through Iowa. The flat ribbon of highway becomes an ordeal that must be endured. But anyone who has lived in Iowa for any length of time knows that the land is neither flat nor boring. Iowa has nuances that cannot be found in her neighboring states of Illinois and Nebraska. Her rolling hills and fertile cornfields offer security. She is a gentle grandmother.

I came to Iowa in 1967 and left in 1973; my goal was a Ph.D. in English. As a direct outgrowth of my Ph.D. dissertation, this book is the culmination of many years of formal schooling. Nevertheless the insights that are most worthy to be passed along are those which have come from the gentle embrace of the Iowa land. This book properly belongs to Iowa and to her living and nonliving spirits—past, present, and future.

For helping me discover the land, I am indebted to the People of the Red Earth. Many years ago, they visited Iowa and decided that it was a good place to live: there the corn grows well, the wildlife is abundant in forests and streams, and the weather is neither too cold in the winter nor too warm in the summer. In Iowa, there is peace.

I thank the Mesquakies for letting me drive up and down the roads of their settlement. And I thank especially those people, some two dozen, who talked to me as a neighbor and a friend. In telling me why they could not reveal their secrets, they forced me to examine more closely my own past. Out of respect for their privacy and their sense of collective identity, I will not mention individual Mesquakies. In the book I have used fictional names and have tried to conceal clan identity. My debt to them is great. I have tried hard to make proper use of the material that was shared with me, and I apologize if I have, through ignorance, violated any sacred promises.

In an entirely different way, I am indebted to my father and mother, who first taught me about the land. The land they farmed was taken from them during the Great Depression, and my father, struggling to make a living as a railroad car inspector, was forever frustrated in his desire to return to the land. His way was different from that of the Mesquakies: his concept of ownership was different; his plow took more than the top six inches; he *used* the land to make a living. It was a way he had learned from his grandfather, who came to this country from Scotland in the same year that the Mesquakies returned from Kansas to Iowa. My father's way clashed violently with the native American way it displaced, and that battle is still raging within my conscience. But I know that my father and his grandfather truly loved the land and respected its goodness. If it had been within their power, they would have been good friends of the People of the Red Earth. Whatever their motive, whatever the result, my ancestors are a part of me I cannot forget.

While I was writing my dissertation, Donna and I lived in several farmhouses among Amish and Mennonite people whose love for the land is equally strong. From these people, we received food, shelter, and good will that sustained us through difficult times. I am especially grateful to Wilbur and Mary Litwiller; in the farmhouse we rented from them I wrote three drafts of my dissertation. Their house has pleasant feelings that we will never forget; from them, I learned much about the land.

There are several people more directly responsible for this book and the dissertation that preceded it. I am indebted to the English Department of the University of Iowa for allowing me to do a dissertation that was outside of traditional scholarly lines but one that I considered personally and culturally valuable. I chose Iowa as a place to do graduate study because I felt the English Department there encouraged creativity as well as scholarship. I was not disappointed. Many of my teachers gave me valuable insights, but I am particularly grateful to Robert Sayre and Harry Oster, who co-directed my dissertation. Sayre spent many hours guiding me step by step, with sensitivity and intelligence, through the writing of my dissertation. His help and encouragement were indispensable.

For allowing me to continue my research into native American history and culture, I am indebted to the Newberry Library and its Center for the History of the American Indian. During the 1973–1974 academic year, the library provided me with a postdoctoral fellowship and the use of its excellent Ayer collection. It was during this time that I started revising my dissertation into a book, and I am grateful for the help and support provided by the library and its staff.

I am most deeply grateful to the two people who helped me reshape my study into a book. Arthur F. Gould, my literary agent, first recognized the potential of the manuscript and provided valuable critical commentary along the way. Anita McClellan, an extremely perceptive editor, guided me patiently through the difficult process of writing a book. Like a true teacher, she always allowed me to find my own path—questioning and probing and helping me to see the fullness of my experience.

Finally, I would like to thank my wife, Donna, who has lived through all of my experiences and with whom I have shared every aspect of my life for the past four years. This is her book as much as mine for our ideas, feelings, and lives are inseparable.

FRED McTAGGART

Kalamazoo, Michigan

Wolf That I Am

◇ 1 ◇

Four years ago, I set out to collect stories from the Mesquakie Indians who live near Tama, Iowa. For two or three days every week, through the fall and winter of 1970 and on into the spring and summer of 1971, I visited the settlement, about 3000 acres of communal property that the Mesquakies chose for themselves along the Iowa River. I talked to people of all ages and eventually became somewhat comfortable with a way of life completely different from my own. I learned something about the Mesquakies and their culture; mainly, I learned about myself.

I did not succeed as a collector and scholar of Mesquakie folklore. I was told a few stories but not nearly as many as I had hoped to find. Many were told to me not as examples of traditional stories but almost as riddles to help me understand something about what I was doing and why. I did not come back to Iowa City with the rich collection of folklore that I sought. Not one single authentic Mesquakie story did I record on tape as proof to my academic advisers that I had completed a scholarly task.

If I had sought only stories, I would have quit early that fall and undertaken a safer and more rewarding academic project. For an entire year, I faced frustration and impatience. Yet, as I look back four years later, I can see that the year I spent traveling to the Mesquakie settlement was one of the most rewarding of my life.

On the Mesquakie settlement, I received an education, al-

2 ◇ WOLF THAT I AM

though it was not a conscious, formal effort on the Indians' part or mine. I had no teacher or guide and I was given no access to esoteric secrets. (Indeed, I learned not to seek such access, at least until I was ready for the experience.) My relationship with the Mesquakies was not special. Some may remember me as the furry-faced man who came asking questions. Others probably have forgotten me. I made little impact, positive or negative, on their daily lives.

But in another sense, my relationship with them was very special, for it is the same relationship they form with any creature who wanders along their roads. They displayed to me their uniqueness, and, indirectly, they reminded me that I too was unique. As separate, finite individuals we met and partook of one another's powers. In the meeting itself, the shared experience, was a teaching.

Before I could learn, I had to realize that I am not and never will be a Mesquakie. They are what they are because of a shared experience that has united them. However, when I quit trying to gain special knowledge, when I quit trying to uncover the secrets of the Mesquakies, I found something a great deal more valuable. I found the secrets that are mine — the secrets that are buried in my past but which can be used in the present and the future. These secrets belong to me; they are also a part of every person who has come to the shores of North America. The meeting that I had with the Mesquakies is one that has taken place and is taking place again and again; the teaching that I received is the same that is given to all visitors by a people who have a special relationship with the land on which we live. Mesquakies told me that my people have forgotten this teaching; I suspect that some never listened. Like all secrets, the teaching must be discovered anew by each traveler.

Since I left Iowa, a major part of my life has been spent writing about the experiences I had. As I write and rewrite, I realize more and more how impossible it is to re-create on the printed page the sacred moments of life. Yet, as I write, the events come back to me with renewed clarity. I relive the experiences and each time I relive them, I gain new insights. These experiences are, I think, a story, perhaps the story I was really seeking when I made my first trip toward the West. This book will be an attempt to tell that story.

◇ **2** ◇

I AM NOT an anthropologist, and I have never been able to
explain adequately to other scholars why I first decided to write
a dissertation on the stories of the Mesquakie Indians. At cock-
tail parties, at job interviews, it is always the first question I am
asked: "How did you get interested in the Indians?" I have finally learned to shrug my shoulders. There are rational answers having to do with my interest in oral traditions. But I
know that these are not the real reasons.

I was completing my Ph.D. in English at the University of
Iowa, and my special interest was folklore. Through Yeats and
Joyce, I had learned to look for the relationships between oral
tradition and literature. Folklore was, I learned, more than a
source of quaint images from a cultural past. But I wanted to
learn more and that could be done, I decided, only through
studying a living oral tradition. I turned to my native American neighbors, eighty miles to the west in Iowa, for an example
of this living oral tradition.

The reason for my decision was simple; the full story behind
it is more difficult to tell. I had suffered through a painful
divorce, then a bitter breakup of a communal day-care group
that had been envisioned as an extended family. For nearly a
year, I experienced an overwhelming sense of isolation.

During that period, I was studying for my Ph.D. examinations, another experience that seemed to break me down into
smaller and smaller parts, to make me into more and more a
specialist with single-minded goals. I argued with my advisers,

questioning the ultimate value of the goals they had set for me. And in doing so, I alienated them and created even more isolation for myself.

I completed my examinations and passed. My academic victory coincided neatly with the final breakup of my marriage. I felt more depressed and more uncertain than ever. In preparing myself for a career, I had created a mess of my life. And now it became apparent that I had not even prepared myself for a career. Teaching jobs were not to be had — especially for those who had alienated their advisers. After spending more than $30,000 and six years of my life following someone else's path, I discovered that the path led right back to myself.

I still had a dissertation to complete, but I did not want to do it unless it could be a positive experience that would help me to learn to live as well as think. I had been attracted to literature because of its qualities of life, and I still wanted to find those qualities. I wanted to find out what it was that imbued words with such power and meaning for so many people.

During a restless summer, I selected and rejected several overworked dissertation topics concerning Yeats and Joyce. And I took a photography course — snapping images and trying to capture them on film. It was during this period that things began to change for me. First, I met my present wife, Donna, and my isolation became transformed into the voluntary seclusion of two lovers. In our romantic illusion, nothing else mattered and I even quit taking pictures. Finally, on a humid night in mid-August, I read *Black Elk Speaks*. My romantic instincts of another sort were aroused. This was a book that lived. It spoke to me and I felt the "intimate contact" that John Neihardt tried to evoke.

The next day, I visited the office of Harry Oster, the folklore specialist at Iowa University, and proposed to write a dissertation on the stories of the Mesquakie Indians. My decision came that quickly. I expected to be talked out of the project, but instead Oster encouraged me. He was an experienced collector himself, and he offered to provide the help and the initial contacts necessary. "I don't know how much of their culture is left," Oster said, "but I'm sure you can find a few older people who still tell stories. You might be able to show how acculturation has made changes in their storytelling process." Oster's office was cluttered with boxes filled with recorded tapes. He was well known for his work collecting folklore from black spiritual singers and Cajuns in Louisiana, from the Amish and Mennonites in Iowa. But he knew very little about American Indians, and he sent me for further help to Bob Sayre, who taught a course in American Indian literature.

Sayre brought me back to reality. "You have a lot of groundwork to do," he cautioned me. "It may be a new field for literature, but it isn't for anthropologists. There are a hell of a lot of books you'll have to read before you can even begin." I knew that, and I had already started to read.

The first meeting with the Mesquakies was planned six weeks hence to give me a chance to absorb as much of this reading material as possible. Oster knew one man from the Mesquakie settlement. Several years ago, he had helped send a Mesquakie drummer, Albert Cloud, to a folk festival in Washington, D.C. To Cloud, Oster sent a letter requesting a meeting with Mesquakie people who had authority to approve my project. "To my knowledge, there are no telephones on the settlement," he said. "So I'll ask him to call me collect before October fifteenth."

For five and a half weeks, we waited for the call. I was becoming extremely anxious. As I pored over the studies of anthropologists Sol Tax and Fred Gearing, I became more and more excited about my project. At least once on the Mesquakie settlement there had been a vital oral tradition and a distinctive culture. I learned that the Mesquakies had preserved their culture better than most tribes. At one time, they were recognized as one of the most conservative American Indian tribes in North America. When they were sent by the United States government to Kansas in 1845, they refused to accept reservation life and returned to Iowa to live on land they chose as their special place. They sold their ponies and possessions to buy the land from white settlers, and they still shared the land in their traditional communal way. As the books put it, the land was a refuge for them. I became more and more convinced that I wanted to learn from the Mesquakies and help them preserve their culture from the encroachment of mass society.

But still no word from Albert Cloud; I was worried that my project might not meet the approval of the Mesquakies. Each day, I checked with Oster, but still no phone call. Finally, in the late afternoon of October 15, he received a short handwritten note from Albert Cloud. Briefly and formally, the note set up a meeting for October 16. The next day.

3

Early on the morning of October 16, Sayre, Oster, and I set out for the Mesquakie settlement. It was a warm day, but the ground was red with fallen leaves. The three of us rode in Oster's older model Mercedes Benz. I had with me some of the more important books and a notebook. In the back seat were Oster's tape recorder and my camera. We had no idea what would take place at the meeting, but we wanted to be equipped.

The two narrow ribbons of Interstate 80 cut through rich, rolling farmland — some of the best in the Midwest. Most of the corn was still standing, but in a few fields the combines were at work, like huge prehistoric animals swallowing the stalks in huge bites. I was vaguely aware that corn is important to American Indian peoples. Would there be combines on the Mesquakie settlement, I wondered. Did they make a living from their land?

A smaller highway, branching north off the interstate, took us into Tama, a duplicate of thousands of other Midwest farming towns. I had been born and raised in such a town, and I knew instinctively how to find my way around — to the high school, the post office, and the other important meeting places. Tama had perhaps more than its share of bars; I spotted four in the main business district. One of my students at the university had grown up in Tama. He warned me: "You'll find plenty of Indians in the bars. They come in to spend their welfare checks." The books had alerted me to expect such racial stereotyping from the white neighbors of the Mesquakies.

On the northwest corner of town, we found a drive-in called the Wigwam, and there we asked directions to the Mesquakie settlement. The waitress looked us over carefully. Each August, hundreds of tourists come to the Mesquakie Powwow to witness Indian dancing and to purchase beadwork. But this was October. I could tell that she didn't trust us, but she pointed straight west. "Stay on the road — about two miles on your right." On the wall of the restaurant were pictures of Black Hawk, Keokuk, and Chief Joseph. None were Mesquakies, but at least Black Hawk and Keokuk had once lived in the same camp with the Mesquakies. Under the suspicious stare of the waitress, we quickly ate our chief burgers, then headed west.

Immediately, the richly cultivated land took on a completely different appearance. There were thick clumps of timber along the road and none of the neatly fenced plots of land that we had seen earlier. We crossed a tributary of the Iowa River, then passed under an old railroad viaduct. A large wooden sign, warped and peeling, directed us to the 1961 Mesquakie Powwow. "It looks like they're about ten years behind the times," one of us remarked.

The dirt road into the settlement was crude, full of deep holes. Oster's Mercedes that had purred so gracefully along the interstate now struggled to avoid the holes, bumping its way from one side of the road to the other, lifting a heavy cloud of dust. I worried about the front suspension.

A thick timber of pine trees lined each side of the road. Every half mile or so, in little clearings set back some distance from the road, we could see the Mesquakie dwellings, mostly small, unpainted houses. In the window of one house was an old hand-painted sign: LAWN MOWERS, SAWS SHARPENED. Alongside many of the houses were open lodges of several types. Some were rectangular; most were small, circular domes made of branches of trees bent double and tied. "Almost like Bucky Fuller domes," Bob Sayre said. We all remarked at the unique construction, obviously traditional yet at the same time very modern in style.

"They're wickiups," I said. My reading had made me an instant expert, and I could feel the others turn their attention toward me for further information. "In English, that's wigwam. These are woodlands Indians, and they didn't live in tepees. They lived in wickiups. I guess many were covered with bark."

"I wonder what they're used for today," Sayre remarked.

"I've heard they're used to store lawn mowers and garden equipment," Oster quipped.

We all chuckled, but it was not intended as a joke. We all assumed that a great deal of acculturation had taken place and the leftover items from a traditional life seemed incongruous.

Suddenly, in a large clearing on our right loomed the Presbyterian Church, a modernistic structure with a traditional European steeple and a traditional native American mosaic on the front. Next door was a white frame house — very similar to the farmhouse I lived in near Iowa City. A white fence surrounded it. It was, I presumed, the home of the minister.

A few miles along the road, in an even larger clearing, was the schoolhouse — a long, one-story structure built on the order of World War II army barracks. In front was a newer sign, still wooden, with large block letters: SAC AND FOX AREA DAY SCHOOOL.

"Are they Sac and Fox? Or are they Mesquakie?"

Again, I was the expert. "They've always been known by the government, and even by anthropologists, as Fox or Sac and Fox. But they call themselves Mesquakie."

"That means 'People of the Red Earth,' doesn't it?" Oster asked.

I nodded. "They've always been separate from the Sacs. But the two tribes were allies and lived in the same camp during the eighteenth and early nineteenth centuries. A few of them intermarried. Black Hawk was a Sac and the Mesquakies weren't officially involved in the Black Hawk War, but the government took away land from both tribes after the war was over. Keokuk was a Sac, too, but he was friendly to the whites and agreed to sell most of the land in Iowa. The treaties were made with the Sac and Fox as if they were one tribe."

"But they're really Mesquakie and not Fox?"

"Yeah." I clutched my books and hoped I hadn't confused my facts. Bob Sayre did not seem convinced.

By now, it was clear that we had no way of finding Albert Cloud's house. Even though each house had a mailbox, the hand-lettered names were faded and hard to read. Some had no names. At the next clearing on the left, Oster pulled the Mercedes over to ask directions. The house was tiny, the smallest we had seen, and a half-dozen dogs surrounded Oster as he walked first to the front door and then the back. From the car, we could see a very old lady open the door. Oster was gesturing emphatically as he talked with her.

On a line strung across the yard were several small, skinned animals. Across the clearing were two outhouses — a swastika was scrawled on one, the names of black musicians Jimi Hendrix and B. B. King were on the other. Sayre and I smiled at the incongruity.

Oster was back in the car. "Strange about some of these little houses," he said. "The front door is always permanently boarded up." He was used to the role of outsider in an isolated folk culture. "The woman could speak only a little English." He leaned toward me in the back seat. "That's a good sign for you. When the language is preserved, then the stories usually are too."

Albert Cloud greeted us at the back door of his house. It was small, but a new wing was under construction at the back. Harry Oster made the introductions and Mr. Cloud smiled shyly and nodded as he shook hands with each of us. He was a small man who looked middle-aged. I learned later that he was sixty-three.

The wickiup behind his house was one of the finest we had seen. "That's really an impressive structure," Oster remarked. "What is it you call it?" I noted his technique. He did not need the information, but he did want Mr. Cloud to talk about the wickiup and its function.

"It's a wickiup," Mr. Cloud said softly.

"Oh, yes. What is it you use them for?"

Cloud acted almost as if he hadn't heard the question. He was motioning us in the door. As we passed by him, he said softly, "Oh, sometimes we put things in them I guess."

Three straight-backed chairs were waiting for us inside the Clouds's living room. The house had looked very small from the outside but now the living room seemed very large. Introductions were formal but cordial; we took our place in the center of the room. On one side Albert Cloud sat with his wife, Ruth, a tall woman with high cheekbones who smiled a great deal but said little. Beside the Clouds was their married daughter, Lucille Waters. She must have been in her forties, for she talked of her college-age daughter. In her blue jeans and Western boots, she could easily have been mistaken for an undergraduate. On the other side of the room were John and Lucy Sturgeon. They were both in their mid-thirties but were still taking classes at the university. In the corner, leaning back on a single bed that had been placed there for double duty as a couch, was a very heavy man with eyes set deeply in his head. He was introduced as James Youngman, the artist, but we had never heard of his work. He smiled, shook hands, then retreated to the couch and said nothing more.

The session was formal but not uncomfortable. John Sturgeon and Lucille Waters did most of the talking, but the Clouds smiled and often nodded agreement. I could not tell what James Youngman was thinking. Once, when I looked his way, he was sleeping. His face was very round and his gray coveralls hugged his body. He did not seem at all like other artists I had known.

As Harry Oster explained the project that I had in mind, the Mesquakies listened closely, often nodding their assent. I was embarrassed at being the center of attention, but I felt pleased that my project was getting such careful attention. The Clouds mentioned the work done by Sol Tax and Fred Gearing. I could not tell if they approved of these anthropologists, but I quickly pointed out that I was not an anthropologist, that I was an English major and that my aims were different.

John Sturgeon looked directly in my eyes and cocked his head slightly to one side. "We do not have departments here," he said. "We see all of life as being related." His voice was very soft, and I did not at first notice what he was trying to tell me.

"I've read some of your stories, and I think they are very beautiful," I said. "I would like to understand them better and to help others see that they are worthwhile."

John's answer was still in a very soft voice, but his gaze was even more intent. "I've studied your culture too," he said. "There are many things that are beautiful and there are some things that are not so beautiful." By now, his criticism was clear. He continued: "Our stories are not intended to be beautiful. Every story has a purpose and that purpose is to teach." I leaned back in my chair to listen. I had been foolish to be so forward, and I was worried that I had destroyed my chances of having my project approved.

Sturgeon released me from his gaze and after a short pause continued in a more impersonal tone. Quietly at first and then growing gradually more emphatic, he began to describe the work of the people who had come to the settlement in the past: William Jones, who was half Mesquakie and could speak the language fluently; Truman Michelson, an anthropologist from the Smithsonian who had angered and amused a few people by publishing religious rituals; Sol Tax, who studied social organization, and his students, who came from the University of Chicago in the 1950s to practice what they called "action anthropology." Eloquently Sturgeon described their work, almost as if he were giving a review of scholarship for a Ph.D. dissertation. Then he looked at me again. "There are over two hundred books written about the Mesquakies. Read them first and then you will be ready to begin."

Mrs. Cloud left the room for a minute and when she returned she handed me a thin booklet entitled *The Mesquakies of Iowa.* As I thumbed through it, I saw that it had been prepared by the University of Chicago anthropologists of the nineteen fifties. "You can keep that, if you like," she said, smiling.

John Sturgeon was talking again, this time in the impersonal tone. He was almost academic in his style, very emphatic, yet had an eloquence that I was not used to hearing. The rhythms and periods of his speech were carefully measured and he punctuated with emphatic hand and head gestures.

"You know," he said, "the government has always encouraged scholars to study Indians. There are many grants given for that purpose. And the people come here and they are all good men. Their motivations are good. They write their books, but they don't know how their work is going to be used.

"Sol Tax is a good man. He came here to make friends and he wrote a book so that people can understand us. It is a good book. But the government can read that book — it is public property — and they can use it to find out how to control us, maybe even how to destroy our culture." He paused for a minute and looked into the distance. "So there are many dilemmas." I nodded emphatically. Now, I felt, we were beginning to establish some understanding.

"That's something that really concerns me," I said. "I want to do something constructive. I want to do something to help your people — or else nothing at all." I assumed that the Mesquakies heard and understood what I said, but I could not be sure. For the next few minutes they talked among themselves in Mesquakie. Now, Mr. and Mrs. Cloud were speaking and even James Youngman awoke from his nap to take part. They were gesturing as they spoke, but I could not figure out either the tone or substance of the conversation. I began to feel uncomfortable.

Then John Sturgeon spoke to me again in English. "I think that what you have in mind could be a very good thing for us," he said.

Lucille Waters leaned forward in her chair. "In the past, many of our people forgot their traditions," she said. "Why, I didn't even take part in dances until recently. Now, I've had to learn about my own culture. Our way is very important to us. If it dies, we have nothing left." I looked at Harry Oster. This was what we had hoped and expected to find.

For the last half-hour or so, the conversation had been accompanied by a steady drumbeat and the chanting of young voices. A group of children, ranging in age from about eight to twelve, had gathered on the back porch. The drumbeat was insistent and the singing became progressively louder until it became a part of our conversation. Lucille Waters pointed toward the porch. "A few years ago, this would not have happened," she said. "Today, our children are determined to preserve their traditions. And we intend to do everything we can to help them."

Mrs. Cloud nodded her agreement. "This is not just for your benefit, either," she said. "Every day, as soon as school is out, we hear them out there on the drum." The singing was becoming louder.

"At the school, the teachers don't do anything," Lucille said.

"It used to be that our children would be disciplined if they spoke their own language in the schoolhouse. We've changed that, but they're still very unfriendly and the teachers don't bring in any Mesquakie culture." She was clearly very angry about the situation, yet still controlled.

"Do you think it would be possible for me to compile a collection of stories that might be used in the school?" I asked. But again, I wasn't sure that I had been heard. Lucille had walked across the room and spoke to John Sturgeon for several minutes in Mesquakie. Then she walked back to her place beside her parents, and John spoke.

"There is a dilemma here. What you want to do is important. But many people will be very reluctant to talk to you. It will be difficult."

"Could you give me some names of people who might be helpful?"

"Some people will talk to you; some won't. You will have to find that out for yourself. But if you are interested in religious stories, you have come to the wrong place. Everyone knows what can be told. There is no question about that. No one has to be told what they can and can't tell you." He paused. "You will just have to find out for yourself."

"What is a religious story?" Bob Sayre asked. "Exactly what is your definition of religion?"

The look in John Sturgeon's eyes was the same as it had been a few minutes before when I had mentioned the difference between English and anthropology. "Religion? There is no such thing." And Sturgeon left us for a minute, confused at this total contradiction, for he had used the word at least fifteen times that morning. We were fumbling for an answer, but before we could respond, he continued. "I use the word only because that is what you can understand. For us, there is no one day of the week, no building for a church. Everything we do is religious. Everything is sacred."

By now, the singing of the children had become so overwhelming that we could not continue to talk. "Do you think they would come in here and sing for us?" Oster asked. "I would really like to get some of that on tape. Then maybe we could talk with the Clouds for a minute. Maybe Mr. Cloud could tell us some stories."

Mr. Cloud shook his head. "I don't remember any stories," he said. The stress was on "stories."

"Oh, that's okay. We'll see," said Oster. "How about it? Can I go get my tape recorder?" No response. Oster looked questioningly around the room, finally accepting the silence as assent. He brought the machine from his car and set it beside his chair, placing the microphone directly in the center of the room. The equipment was expensive and professional; it turned the Clouds's austere living room into a recording studio. At this point, James Youngman excused himself and left, awkwardly smiling and backing out the door. "He has to get back to his artwork," Mrs. Cloud said, and the others laughed loudly.

Finally, the children, with coaxing from Oster, started again on the drum, which they had placed directly in front of the microphone. Shyly at first, they sang, in whining, high-pitched voices. One boy started and then the others joined in, imitating his voice and at the same time singing around and against it. Gradually, their voices became sharper, more plaintive, blending together behind the steady beat of the drum. I could feel the drum pounding within me. There was something extremely exciting about their chants, and when they were finished, my heart was pounding uncontrollably. I felt drained, as if I had been singing along with them. It was a very moving experience.

Without a word, the children picked up their drum and left. But their presence was felt for several minutes as we sat in silence. Finally, John Sturgeon spoke: "That is part of our problem. That was a Sioux song. The children hear these songs at the Powwow. The songs have a good rhythm and a good sound. They like the beat and they sing them. It is okay. But for us, the songs have no meaning."

I leaned forward in my chair, prepared to speak. I knew now that I could do something to help the Mesquakies preserve their culture. I was anxious to get started. Sturgeon must have noticed my reaction. Before I could answer, he spoke again: "What I have just said is true." He then extended his right hand in an emphatic gesture of qualification. "But there is another side to that. The children are singing Sioux songs because there are strangers in the room, and they are reluctant to sing their own Mesquakie songs before strangers."

Again, I was confused. Throughout the day, Sturgeon had repeatedly given me what seemed to be contradictory messages. On the one hand he was saying that Mesquakie traditions needed to be recorded lest they be lost. Then in the next breath he seemed to be holding me back — warning me that some of the material could not be given to me because it was too sacred. I did not know what to think, but it was clear that Sturgeon was not willing to spell out his position with any more precision. His point had been made and he leaned back in his chair.

Harry Oster had moved the microphone over to where the Clouds were sitting, and he was attempting, with some success, to interview them. Mr. Cloud was especially uncomfortable, but I took it as shyness. I had watched Oster in action before and I knew that if anyone could get Mr. Cloud to relax in front of the microphone, Oster was the one.

Mr. Cloud still insisted that he remembered no stories, but he was talking about his childhood: "When I was young, I was brought up very different from what you are used to. I was taught that everything is sacred — the animals, the birds, the trees, even rocks." He was, I felt sure, a potential Black Elk who could tell a moving and beautiful story. "I was taught not to fear the weather but to welcome it. When it would rain or snow or when the winds would blow, I was taught to go out and welcome the weather." He was speaking slowly; even though he was using perfect English, it was not easy for him. "I was taught that all things are related." He swung his arm in a wide arc.

"Did you ever go through any initiations?" Oster asked.

Cloud nodded. "When the ice formed on the river, I was told to go break the ice and swim in the river." He paused. "And I was told to fast . . ."

Oster interrupted. "What happened to you when you fasted?" He too had just read *Black Elk Speaks* and it appeared that he was on the trail of a valuable story.

Cloud sat silent for several minutes. Then Oster repeated the question, for it appeared that Cloud had not heard or understood. "What happens to you when you fast?"

Very slowly, Cloud answered: "Well . . . first you get hungry . . ."

Oster, Sayre, and I laughed uproariously at the straight-faced joke; I did not notice if the Mesquakies were laughing. Oster started putting aside his tape recorder. By now, we were very hungry and tired. We had been talking for almost six hours.

Mrs. Cloud served us coffee — the blackest, strongest coffee I had ever tasted. And the three of us took turns racing to the outhouse to release our cramped bladders. Oster put away his equipment, as we prepared to leave. We had been welcomed to the Mesquakie settlement. I was anxious to get started on my project and assured them I would be back the following Friday. "When you do, come back and see us," Mrs. Cloud said warmly.

Outside, Oster grabbed the camera from the back seat of the car and shot three quick pictures of the wickiup outside the Cloud house. It had been a productive day and we were all ecstatic as we left. Stopping at the Wigwam, we stuffed ourselves with chief burgers before heading back to Iowa City.

4

THE TAPE that was made that first day belonged to Harry Oster, and I never heard it again. However, the most important things that happened had not been recorded on tape. All of the scenes came back vividly to me and I reconstructed them time and again for Donna and my sons, Duncan and Brendan. As I tried to capture the mood and intensity of that meeting, the Clouds became exotic figures, and, in my imagination, I could see them patiently teaching me to understand and tell all the old stories. From Harry Oster's example, I thought I knew how to open them up and get them used to the tape recorder. I was confident that soon they would start to remember stories.

It was important to have a good tape recorder in order to record the stories accurately. For a week, Donna and I wandered through sound stores in Iowa City, but the quality machines cost more than our combined salaries as teaching assistants for a whole year. Actually, we could not afford even the inexpensive cassette models. Perhaps because we looked more like graduate students than faculty members, the audio-visual department at Iowa would not let me borrow a machine, even when I explained my project thoroughly. After a week of worry and frustration, I was getting desperate — I saw no way that I could collect stories without a tape recorder. Then finally, the night before I was due to return to the settlement, a friend offered to loan me a professional-model tape recorder. The controls were complicated, but after a long evening of practice I thought I knew how to operate it.

Early Friday morning, I packed the clumsy machine into my

Ford Falcon station wagon and headed for Tama. It was an extremely warm day, and it was easy to forget that it was already mid-October. Yet as soon as I passed the warped 1961 Powwow sign, the colors of fall became overwhelming. It was indeed a new land, and even the familiar sights from a week earlier stood out in exotic contrast. As I passed Mesquakies walking down the bumpy dirt road, they waved at me, without expression. I wondered if they knew who I was, if they remembered me from the week before.

I had made an appointment for 9:00 A.M. with the Clouds, but when I arrived, only Mrs. Cloud was at home. She was friendly, yet nervous and somewhat preoccupied. "My husband is not here," she explained, "but he will be back in a few minutes." I sat down in the chair that had been occupied by John Sturgeon. It was an awkward wait. We smiled at each other, and I tried to carry on a conversation but with little success. The tape recorder was an embarrassing lump beside my chair.

About thirty minutes later, Mr. Cloud returned with his son, a man about thirty-five years of age. Now we were ready to begin, but the awkwardness was still present. We sat looking at one another. For me, at least, the silence was devastating. I talked about the weather, and Mr. Cloud smiled and nodded. More silence. Finally, Mrs. Cloud noticed my embarrassment and tried to help. "It's Indian Summer," she said with a short laugh.

"I wonder how that got started?" I asked.

More silence. Then Mr. Cloud answered: "I think I know how it got started." He seemed a bit angry, yet he did not continue as I expected. I sat, leaning forward in my chair, waiting to hear how it got started. Finally, he continued: "People say that when Indians say something, they do not mean it. It's an Indian promise." It was not a joke, and I was sorry I had brought up the subject of the weather.

Awkwardly, I tried to remind the Clouds of our visit the week before. I asked about the grandchildren. They both smiled, but the silence continued. Again, it was Mrs. Cloud who finally spoke. "You're interested in stories, aren't you?"

"Yes, I am." My voice was, I am sure, too eager.

She smiled, but gave no further response.

"I can't remember any stories," Mr. Cloud said with a wave of his hand. More silence, then he continued: "It has been too long. I can't remember." He was smiling and I sensed that he was trying hard to be courteous.

The tape recorder was on the floor to my left. Mr. Cloud's son, Raymond, was in the straight chair directly to my right.

"Would you like to talk about anything else?" I asked.

Mr. Cloud shook his head.

Suddenly, Raymond Cloud began to talk about the anthropologists who had visited them in the past. "Do you know Mr. Sol Tax?"

I nodded. "I know of his work. I have not met him."

"He was pretty good. He came and asked people a lot of questions. But he knew how far he could go. He didn't ask us about religion and that was good."

"I'd like to do the same thing," I said. "I want to learn about stories, but I don't want religious stories. I'm interested in secular stories."

All three of the Clouds nodded and smiled.

"Do you know any secular stories?" I was looking at Mr. Cloud.

Again, he shook his head. "I don't remember any," he said with a shy smile.

Again, Raymond Cloud started talking. "The people who came in the 1950s. Fred Gearing was one of them." It suddenly struck me that this man was too young to know Sol Tax, who had done his field work in the 1930s, but he seemed to talk about all of the anthropologists as if he knew them from personal contact.

"That book I gave you last week," Mrs. Cloud reminded me. "That was put together by Fred Gearing."

"How did people feel about him?"

"Oh, they thought he was fine," said the younger Cloud. "But you know those books he put together, they are still sitting around. He intended for them to be sold at the Powwow but no one did it. They are still sitting around in boxes."

I was puzzled. "Did people not like the book?"

"No, I think it was pretty good," said Mrs. Cloud. "I think most people were upset because they weren't consulted about it. They didn't have any say in how it was to be distributed. So they didn't do anything about it." I couldn't tell if she was criticizing her people or the anthropologists. I finally decided she was doing neither.

Raymond Cloud was still talking about anthropologists. "A man came to me a couple of weeks ago. From the Smithsonian. He was interested in changes in our language."

I jumped at the opportunity to talk about language. "I'd really like to learn your language. Do you think anyone would be willing to teach me?"

"It would be very hard for you. Our language is very difficult for an outsider to learn. It is very different from your language. For example, we might talk about someone or something and never mention it. You would not know what was being talked about — even if you knew what the words meant. But we would know from the context."

The elder Clouds were smiling and nodding agreement. I felt that the room was warming up a bit. Raymond Cloud was, it seemed, trying to interpret for me the reasons his parents were not cooperating with me. All three of the Clouds seemed extremely anxious not to offend me, yet they were not as open as they had been the previous week. It was not easy, and even Raymond seemed awkward in the presence of strangers. But at least we were beginning to establish some mutual understanding.

We continued to talk about the language. I asked the Mesquakie word for "story," for "legend," and for "tell." The elder Clouds responded readily with the definitions I sought but gave no further information. Even though they were friendly now, I was confronted again and again with a silence that I did not understand. I am shy and quiet myself, but this silence was extremely embarrassing for me. After a few minutes, I excused myself and left.

"Do you know anyone who might be able to tell me some stories?" I asked at the door. Mr. Cloud shook his head. Mrs. Cloud paused, then answered. "Go talk to our daughter. She lives just down the road, the next house. Maybe she can tell you who to talk to."

It was still early morning when I made my way to Lucille Waters' house. She was not home, but on the front stoop of her house I talked with her husband, John. "No, she went into town," he said. "I don't know when she'll be back." His voice was very slow and deliberate. He was wearing a blue baseball cap that only partially shielded his eyes from the sun, which was shining directly over my shoulder and into his front door.

"I wanted to ask her if she knew who I might talk to about stories."

"Oh, I don't know." He looked into the distance and his voice trailed off as if it were following his purposeless gaze. "She should be back sometime. I just don't know." I sensed a deliberate vagueness that I had seen so many times among older black people in the ghetto of Saint Louis.

I introduced myself and told him more about my project. "Oh, that's good," he said, pulling his cap down to shade his eyes. "Sounds good."

"Do you know anyone who might help me out?" I could sense myself trying to imitate his casual manner.

"No, I don't. I don't know. Oh, maybe you could talk to John Buffalo. He might tell you some stories."

My ears perked up. I wanted to know more about this man. "Is he known as a storyteller?" John Waters nodded slowly. "Does he know a lot about your culture?"

For the first time, John Waters dropped his mask of indifference. He seemed angry. "No! I don't think he knows anything at all about our culture. He's a Christian. He goes to the Church but he doesn't come to our ceremonies. I doubt if he knows very much at all anymore." He spat along the side of the step and adjusted his baseball cap. His anger was gone as quickly as it had come.

Now I was totally confused. "Well, why did you say he would be a good storyteller?" I decided he must have been joking, and I started to smile. But he wasn't joking.

"No, he *is* a good storyteller. He does a lot of speaking before church and school groups around. I think he'd probably give you some help." The mask was back; I was more confused than ever.

John Waters was looking off into the distance. He changed the subject with a suddenness that surprised me. "You know, when we Indians have a question or problem, we go to the woods and fast — sometimes we go for four days or more. In that way, an answer can be given to us." I could not understand it; one minute he had been hiding from me, the next he was volunteering information about his religion. I listened as he told how important his religion is to him. "We still have our own language, you know, and our old religion. They are very important to us. When we go to Powwows, other tribes tell us, 'You are ten years behind the times.' And we say, 'Yes, maybe we are ten years behind the times.' But now those people are sorry. They have lost their language and their religion, but we still have ours."

He was talking readily and I did not want to interrupt him.

However, I also knew that he was a person worth interviewing, a person I wanted to get on tape. As he talked, my mind kept wandering to the machine lodged in the back seat of the station wagon. When he paused for a moment, I seized the opportunity. "I think you would be a very good person to interview. I really like your way of talking and you have a lot to say. Would you mind if I get the tape recorder from the car?"

"Oh no," he said quickly. "I don't talk very well. You don't want to interview me."

"You're being too modest. You talk very well." I knew now that all he needed was some coaxing. I had seen Harry Oster use the same technique on reluctant informants.

But John Waters would not yield. "No, no. I can't. I really don't have time." Until now, of course, he had been speaking to me very leisurely. But even after further coaxing, he would not change his mind. "Go talk to John Buffalo," he said again. "Maybe he can help you out."

The sun was high in the sky when I left John Waters. It was lunchtime, my stomach told me, but I did not want to travel back into town.

At the top of the hill, I found a house with a large clearing and a sign at the front welcoming tourists. In the clearing were a tepee and a bark wickiup — not to store lawn mowers but to show non-Indian visitors the old way of life. As I got out of my car, a heavyset woman came out of the frame house to greet me. She was carrying a drawer full of beadwork — again for the visitors. It was beautiful work and I knew it would sell for two or three times her price in Iowa City. As I carefully selected a headband to take back to Donna, I tried to establish a conversation with the woman. She seemed totally uninterested in talking about the weather; finally, I told her I was a student from the university and that I was trying to learn about Mesquakie stories. She smiled and nodded. "Do you know anyone who is known as a good storyteller?" I asked.

"John Buffalo," she said quickly. "He is the only one I know of." She straightened up her drawer of beadwork and turned back toward the house. I knew now that John Waters had not been joking, but I was still confused.

In a modern mobile home on the other side of the settlement, I found the Tama Indian Crafts Association. A tall middle-aged woman with straight black hair welcomed me into her trailer, an extremely modern three-bedroom model. On the wall facing the door was a large picture of Jesus, so large and so prominent that it embarrassed me. I remembered John Waters' anger when he talked about Christianity; Lucille had told me a week before that only five or six Mesquakies had joined the church. Now here I was in the home of a Christian.

But as the woman hurriedly brought out a full selection of ceramic tiles silk-screened with traditional Indian designs, she did not seem at all defensive or isolated. She talked freely about the artists as if they were her friends. "This one is from a drawing by James Youngman. Do you know him? He is an excellent artist. He always does this kind of work." She seemed very acculturated, yet very much at home on the settlement.

I told her about my project, hoping she would volunteer to tell me stories or direct me to a good storyteller. She was talkative — a welcome relief from the silence I had experienced earlier that day.

"Oh, I can't help you," she said. "I'm half Sioux and half French myself. If my husband were here, he might tell you someone to talk to. He is Mesquakie. The only person I know of is John Buffalo. I think you should talk to him. He would be perfect." John Buffalo had been following me around all day. Christian though he was, I must talk to him. Maybe he *was* a good storyteller.

The tiles were three dollars each and it was difficult for me to make a decision. Apparently the woman saw my problem. "You're a student, aren't you? I can let you have them for two dollars each." Then, after a short pause: "Well, I can let you have them for a dollar each, but that is as low as I can go." She left for a few minutes and came back with a huge stack of tiles. "These are flawed just a bit. We can't sell them. You can have any of these for free." I was overwhelmed by her generosity. And a bit embarrassed.

As I was preparing to leave, four young children — about the same age as those at the Cloud house — stormed into the house. School was over for the day, and they ran for the kitchen. As they made sandwiches, they sang — soft but high-pitched chants like those I had heard a week before. The woman smiled. "They love to sing," she said.

The afternoon was late, but I decided I must make an attempt to see John Buffalo. At least, I could make an appointment for next week. At a small house down the road, I asked directions. The man was short and heavyset with a bulbous nose. "John Buffalo? I think he is in the hospital. Didn't he have a heart attack? Anyway, I am sure he is in the hospital — maybe even in Davenport."

"Do you know anyone who might be a good storyteller?"

"No, I don't. Maybe you should talk to the minister up the road. You know, at the Presbyterian Church. He could tell you about John Buffalo too."

Of course, I did not want to hear Mesquakie stories from a white Presbyterian minister. I was confused, frustrated, disappointed. I had spent a long day and had nothing except a beaded headband and a stack of tiles to show for it.

I was hungry and stopped at the Wigwam before heading back to Iowa City. At this time of day the place was crowded with high school students, and I waited some time before I was served. As I hurried out of the restaurant, I was already taking a huge bite out of my chief burger.

WOLF THAT I AM ◊ 29

I was astonished by the sudden firm grip on my right biceps. I jumped, then looked around to see James Youngman. I had two of his paintings on ceramic tiles in the back seat of my car.

There was mock anger on his face. "Hey, you need a shave," he said. Then he laughed heartily and waved at me as he strode into the restaurant.

◇ 5 ◇

M‌Y EARLY ENTHUSIASM had been shattered. The Clouds would not tell me stories. Other Mesquakies steered me toward Christianized Mesquakies or the white minister. At this rate, I would never find traditional stories. Harry Oster told me to be patient. Soon I would find a good informant and all my problems would be over. He had faced the same situation many times. But I was not so sure. I sensed my inadequacy as a collector of folklore and seriously considered dropping the project and writing a safer, more traditional dissertation — one based on books rather than people.

I spent a week in the safety of the library reading about the Mesquakies. There I was comfortable and unthreatened. Yet when I left campus, it was always the personal experience that seemed most important. At bedtime, Duncan and Brendan begged me to tell them about the Indians I had met that first day. Friends and neighbors had a similar curiosity, merely channeled into more adult questions. How did the Indians live? Were they happy? Had they accepted me? My topic was exotic. I was doing, it seemed, what many Americans want to do: visiting the Indians and learning the truth that has for so long been hidden behind a cloud of mystery. I enjoyed being the center of attention but was uneasy when faced with questions that I now knew were not easy to answer. The cloud of mystery had become for me a heavy curtain.

If I was to discover anything worthwhile, my real work had

to be done in person. The stories and ethnographic data about the Mesquakies had been compiled many years ago. I had to find out which stories were still living, how they were told, how people felt about them.

Bob Sayre suggested that I talk to James North, a young Mesquakie man enrolled as a freshman at the University of Iowa. As a poet, North seemed to be the ideal person to help me reconcile my reading and my field work. I made an appointment to meet him in the snack bar of the Iowa Memorial Union.

When I arrived, North was waiting for me, his elbows resting heavily against the table. He was almost as heavy as James Youngman. His long black hair was pulled back tightly and tied, highlighting his round face. He was wearing jeans, Western boots, and a navy pea jacket. He had been sketching in a spiral notebook and showed me the drawing he was working on. It was a bit abstract but in the traditional style of other Mesquakie artists.

I was in my environment and James, a poet and an English major, was part of that environment. I felt that I could talk freely without worrying about cultural differences. I munched on peanuts as I explained to him what I wanted to do and why I thought it was important. "Do you have any suggestions about how I should go about it?" I asked.

"Well, I really don't know," he said. "There are people who know stories. I've heard them, but I can't remember them very well." I offered him peanuts, salted in the shell, but he shook his head vigorously. "In fact, I've been meaning to go to my grandmother's house and get her to put some stories on tape so I'll have them when she is gone. If I ever do that, I'll pass them on to you. But I haven't done it yet." I could not tell how serious he was; I doubted that I would ever get from him recorded tapes of his grandmother.

"So your grandmother knows stories?"

"Yes, she knows many stories. Some people know some things; other people know other things."

"Do you think she would talk to me about stories?"

"No." The silence was awkward but he did not want to be discourteous. "She doesn't speak English very well," he said.

"Who is your grandmother?"

He seemed not to hear my question. "You know there is one story I can remember," he said. "I'm not sure, but I think it goes like this:

> There were two Raccoons and a Deer. And I guess one of the Raccoons shat in the other one's eyes. Then the Raccoon went to the river, but he couldn't get across. So he asked the Deer, "Can you carry me to the other side?"
>
> "I don't have any room on my back," said the Deer. So the Raccoon asked if he could ride inside his ass.
>
> "All right," said the Deer, "but don't eat anything."
>
> So the Deer started to swim across the water with the Raccoon inside his asshole. Pretty soon, the Raccoon got hungry and he started to eat. He ate his way up through the Deer's body to his heart and the Deer died.
>
> But so did the Raccoon.

It was my first real Mesquakie story, and I was disappointed not to have my tape recorder handy. I had seen a story like it in a printed collection of Mesquakie stories made by anthropologist William Jones in 1901 and 1902. Yet North's version was obviously garbled. In the printed version, a mouse had ridden inside a deer. That made sense; this story did not.

James North was still looking at me, as if he were trying to read my feelings. He seemed to know that I did not understand the story he had told me.

"Do you have any idea what the story means?" I asked.

I did not expect the straightforward answer that I received: "Don't be too open or people will take advantage of you."

Later that afternoon, I reported my first authentic Mesqua-kie story to Harry Oster. It was, he agreed, an excellent ex-ample to show the acculturative changes that were taking place on the settlement. He reassured me and told me to continue looking for a good informant. "It makes your task all the more important," he said.

"There is just one thing that worries me," I told him. "I keep feeling that North was using the story to tell me someth-ing — like a parable. Do you think that could be true?"

"Oh, I don't know," Oster said. "Maybe if you get to know him better, you can ask him if he was doing that."

◇ 6 ◇

When I returned to the Mesquakie settlement that week-end, we made it a family outing. I left the tape recorder behind and we packed a picnic lunch to eat along the way. I was particularly happy to have Donna and the boys for company to break those long minutes of silence that I expected.

The trip was a crucial one. I wanted to talk to Lucille Waters and find out if I should continue my project. I did not want to irritate the Mesquakies or invade their privacy. If I was unwanted, I would quit now; if not, I needed help in finding people willing to talk to me.

It was another warm day in late October. The breeze was cool but a bright sun made everything pleasant. Lucille greeted us outside her house, and the three of us sat on a fallen log in the front yard while Duncan and Brendan played with the children who had performed so admirably on the drum two weeks earlier. For the children, apparently, the cultural barriers were not so great; very quickly they were playing together contentedly.

Lucille's daughter was home for the weekend. "I'd like both of you to meet her," Lucille said, smiling. "I think you would get along just fine." But the daughter was in town for the afternoon. "She's reading *Black Elk Speaks* in her literature class — and *The Autobiography of Malcolm X,*" Lucille said. "She brought the books home and you know what — I've been reading them!" She smiled proudly. "Parents have a lot to learn too."

As we talked, I could see that this situation was so much more natural than those I had set up earlier. It was not just the absence of a tape recorder. We were meeting as families and what we had to say was neither small talk nor significant information. It was a visit.

Lucille explained that this was a good day for her to talk with us. "But you should always tell people ahead of time that you're coming," she said. "We have fall ceremonies coming up and I'll be busy every Saturday for the next few weeks." Then she reminded me again, "But of course, our ceremonies are not held on one day of the week like yours, so it's always best to check with us ahead of time."

Dogs raced around the clearing in front of us. They were strange-looking dogs, with bloodlines like none I had ever seen. There seemed to be several families of them, and a relatively new litter of puppies ventured out now and then from their home under the house. "Can we have a puppy?" Duncan asked, tugging at my arm. Lucille acted as if she had not heard the question.

"You know our dogs have Indian names," she said. "We name them after the clan we belong to. My husband is a member of the Fish clan and most of our dogs are named after creatures which live in the water and come up to the surface for air. But my son, that boy there, he couldn't seem to keep a dog. All of his dogs kept dying. So he named his next dog after the Thunder clan — my clan — and that dog has lived."

Duncan had already forgotten his request and was off playing again, but Lucille had answered his question. Dogs were relatives of the people, with names and clans. I remembered reading about the special relationship that had been established between Mesquakies and their dogs. The dogs had been with them for many years and in religious ceremonies dogs were sacrificed and eaten in something akin to the Christian communion. Many American Indian tribes have given up the practice of eating dog, I have been told. Mesquakies have not. One man later told me: "I'm sure you have heard that we eat dog. We are very upset that white people found out about that. It is sacred to us and we don't appreciate having people make fun of our religion."

State of Iowa officials may or may not know of these religious practices, but they do consider the dog population on the settlement to be a potential health hazard. At least once a year they set up rabies-innoculation clinics at the day school; one had been held just that morning. Lucille laughed as she recalled an anecdote. "You know that boy, he's always having a time. This morning when he took his dogs in to be inoculated, the man wanted to know the dogs' names. Well, he figured it was none of that man's business, asking after the dogs' names. So he told him his dogs were named Spiro and Nixon. The man said, 'You must be kidding!' but my son said, 'No, honest, that's their names — Spiro and Nixon!'" She laughed heartily. "That man just didn't understand about family names."

Donna and I laughed with her, but I felt a bit uneasy hearing about the jokes played on the outsider.

"Have you ever heard of a man called Michelson?" Lucille asked. "He was an anthropologist from the Smithsonian."

I had just checked his book out of the library and from it I had learned the details of the dog feast ceremony. I nodded hesitantly.

"Well, people played a trick on him many years ago. He came around here asking questions, all kinds of nosy questions about our religion."

I nodded.

"So I guess people wanted to get rid of him, and they told him a *good* story. You know that 'White Owl Sacred Pack'?"

I knew it.

"I guess he paid a lot of money for that." She laughed heartily and I tried to laugh with her. Donna was laughing too, and

I was beginning to feel ganged up on. "He carried those old cow bones all the way to Washington, D.C. I hear they are in a museum somewhere in Europe now and people still go there and worship those old cow bones." By now, the joke was too good to ignore.

I had read "The White Owl Sacred Pack." Truman Michelson and Alanson Skinner had debated the authenticity of that sacred bundle for several months in anthropological journals. Skinner had of course recognized it as a hoax and Michelson finally admitted that it might be. It was a fascinating debate, but that was more than fifty years ago and Lucille Waters was talking about it as if it had happened yesterday. To her Michelson was not a name but a living person.

Her anecdote seemed to confirm what anthropologists had written: the Mesquakies were a deeply conservative people who parted with their traditions reluctantly, if at all. If their religion and their sacred bundles were so important to them, it was highly likely that many of their stories were still intact — still told as they had been told to William Jones in 1900 and 1901.

However, Lucille's story about Truman Michelson bothered me. Her indirection was becoming less subtle, and I felt that it was a good time to state my feelings.

"You know, I don't want to be like Michelson," I said. "Am I being too nosy?" I expected a quick denial, a polite pat on the back. Instead there was no reaction, either positive or negative. She was waiting to hear what I had to say. "I really don't want to embarrass people or get too inquisitive about their religion. In fact, I don't want religious stories at all. I'm interested in secular stories — animal stories or whatever. Something people tell to each other for entertainment. But if I'm embarrassing people or disturbing their privacy, I will quit right now. I just don't want to do that."

Her answer was as direct as any I had been given so far by

Mesquakies. She looked off toward the pine trees to the west, toward her father's house. "You know, my father was not happy last week when Professor Oster had him talk into the tape recorder. But he did not tell him anything important. He just talked. He just told him what he wanted to hear. And that is the way with most white people who come here — we tell them what we think they want to hear.

"If you want that kind of information, you can go to John Buffalo. He tells white people what they want to hear. And I guess he believes some of it himself. But that is not Mesquakie. If you want to know what the Mesquakie think about things, it will not be easy." She was looking first at me and then at Donna. I was happy that Donna had come along, for I suspected that she would not have been as open with me had I come alone.

"But I think you are different, don't you think so?" she asked, looking at Donna for an answer. "I think you are not like those professors. I think you want to know what we are really like, and I think you will succeed in what you are trying to do. But you have to have patience. You have to let us get used to you — how do you say? — let yourself *grow* on us." We laughed at this figure of speech.

"There are many people here who could tell you stories," she continued. "Why, my father could tell you so many stories — if he would. But he is not sure what you are trying to do or why. Don't push things too quickly. Let us get to know you first and then maybe you will learn some stories."

At that point, we were interrupted. Duncan and Brendan were both tugging at my arm. "I have to go to the toilet," Duncan said. He was pointing toward the outhouse across the clearing.

"There is a bathroom in the house," Lucille said.

"No, I want to go to *that* one," he said, pointing across the yard.

She laughed. "It's more romantic that way," she said.

I took the boys to the toilet. For me, it was not romantic; I had used those things for the first twelve years of my life. While I was gone, I learned later, Lucille continued to talk to Donna. She explained to her that many Mesquakie stories were about animals, that they were very funny, but that they were very serious in purpose. They were not intended for mere entertainment. I did not hear any of this, but as we were leaving the outhouse, a rabbit scurried across the clearing in front of us, then ran into the timber.

When I returned, Lucille and Donna were chatting peacefully. The tension that I had felt on my last visit was by now completely gone, and I was excited about my project. Lucille was talking again about her daughter and about Malcolm X. I was still confused, trying to reconcile the bathroom and the outhouse, Truman Michelson and Malcolm X. Those friends and neighbors who asked all the questions would never understand. Yes, the Mesquakies are acculturated. No, they are not acculturated.

But I still wanted the information I had come for. "If you think it is all right for me to continue to ask people about stories, then who should I talk to? Do you know anyone who would be willing to talk to me?"

"Have you tried Henry Sturgeon?" she asked. "He knows a lot; I really respect him. And he also speaks English well. He worked in Marshalltown for many years and is now retired. So I think he understands your people, but he knows a lot about his own people."

"Does he have time to talk? I don't want to waste his time."

"He is retired, and I think he would appreciate having the company, somebody to talk to during the day. But then you will have to ask him that yourself."

The sun had moved behind the pine trees to the west, and we could feel the chill of evening coming on. We had to get back to Iowa City, but Duncan and Brendan were tugging at us again. "We want to take a walk," they said, pointing toward the woods. I looked at Lucille and she nodded. She smiled at the boys. "There are many animals in those woods," she said.

Donna, the boys, and I walked by ourselves down a narrow, winding path through the woods. It was dark and cool inside and within a minute or two we seemed completely lost from the familiar clearing. It was romantic and at the same time frightening. A thick carpet of pine needles lined the path and we made our way noisily along. We saw no animals, but after a short walk we came upon another clearing. It was the home of Mr. and Mrs. Cloud, the parents of Lucille Waters.

We retraced our steps through the woods, got into our car, and returned to Iowa City. It was cold and dark by the time we arrived.

◦ 7 ◦

In the library, I continued to read the texts collected by Truman Michelson — but now with more discrimination and doubt. His list of publications was impressive, and I could tell that most were authentic, detailed, and thorough. With hindsight, it was easy to detect the suspicious tone of "The Owl Sacred Pack of the Fox Indians." But there was, I suspect, some defensiveness in Lucille Waters's reaction. Michelson's books outlined the rituals and ceremonies of the Mesquakies in stark detail. Even though I knew her feelings, I felt compelled to read the books, to dig out the secrets. I too wanted to penetrate the cloud of mystery. More often, however, I found the books to be boring recitals of archaic ritual. I had to force myself to read them, often falling asleep in the easy chair of the library lounge.

In one text, I was startled to come across a name familiar to me: John Buffalo. I still had not met the man, but his name continued to follow me. Michelson's book was published in 1916; Buffalo must by now be very old. He was, Michelson explained, a very educated man and a member of the Presbyterian Church, but he was also a participant in some of the most important Mesquakie religious rituals, and in the book he revealed details about these ceremonies, including the names and locations of the participants.

In later texts, Michelson did not reveal the names of his informants because, as he said, some had been ostracized by the tribe for giving away religious secrets. I wondered if the feelings expressed by the Waters were part of an ostracism that had begun fifty-five years earlier. I was shocked at the seeming persistence of the Mesquakie memory, the fierce determination to preserve religious secrets. What was it about their religion that must be kept so closely guarded? It was a trait I could not understand.

Michelson's books were only vaguely related to my purposes. Much more interesting and relevant was the collection of stories, *Fox Texts,* compiled by William Jones in 1901 and 1902. Jones was born of a half Mesquakie father and an English mother, but he was raised by his grandmother, Katiqua, a full-blooded Mesquakie of the Eagle clan. Until he was nine, Megasiawa, or Black Eagle, as he was known on tribal rolls, was raised in the traditional manner in a bark lodge on the Sac and Fox Reservation in Oklahoma. He learned Mesquakie and was told the stories and traditions of his people. However, when his grandmother died, Jones was sent to Hampton Institute in Virginia, where he was graduated with honors. He then attended Harvard and Columbia, studying anthropology under famous scholars. He was a student of Franz Boas when he returned to Iowa to conduct "linguistic and ethnological investigations" among the Mesquakies.

There, as he revealed in his notebooks, he was introduced by his father and welcomed as a member of the Eagle clan. He was allowed inside the ceremonial lodges and told:

> We let you inside the lodge because you are one of us — not one of our clan, but one of our people. One thing only we ask of you; it is that you remove your hat and your coat before you enter the lodge. Leave them behind. The reason is plain: the manitous are inside the place . . . No one is there with hat and coat, everybody is in appropriate dress. So what we ask is merely for the purpose of removing the fear of disturbing the peaceful presence of the manitous.

The stories Jones collected were heard from Mesquakies in a natural context over a period of many months. In the introduction to *Fox Texts*, he explains that "what was imparted was done in friendship and by way of a gift, not all at once, but at leisure and bit by bit . . . Every single piece of text was told but once, and delivered without thought of the purpose I meant to make of the material." He reiterates what I had already discovered: Mesquakies are very reluctant to part with any traditional stories.

Jones, however, was more sensitive than most scholars to the desires of the people who helped him. Some information about ceremonial practices he put in his notebooks but never published. It is rumored that he put some of the most sensitive material in a sealed envelope that was not to be opened until all the old people had died. That envelope has never been found, but scholars are still searching. Jones himself was killed at a very young age while doing field work in the Philippines.

Fox Texts is a scholarly format: texts in the Mesquakie language with a bald, literal translation on the facing page. The book was intended for linguists, and I found in it none of the "intimate contact" that I had sensed in *Black Elk Speaks*. Many texts were as difficult to read as those of Michelson. Yet, as I read them, some of the stories took on an unexplainable vitality and gave me a feeling for the people Jones had talked to.

One of these was the story of "The Raccoon and the Wolf." As I read it in the stacks of the University of Iowa library, I felt a sense of closeness and I wanted to understand the story more fully. Perhaps William Jones had a particularly meaningful relationship with the anonymous teller of the story and that relationship somehow was transmitted through the words on the page. Perhaps the story summed up for me an insight about my early experiences on the Mesquakie settlement. Whatever the reason, the story has become very important to me. Even though my understanding of it is limited, I have returned to it again and again for the past four years.

A Wolf was passing along when lo! he met a Raccoon. "Ah, and so my younger brother is out for a walk over the country?" said he to him.

"Yes," said the Raccoon.

"Whither are you going, my dear younger brother?" said the Wolf.

"Oh, to yonder place where the river goes flowing across country," said the Raccoon.

"Oh, my dear little brother, I wonder if you have with you anything in the way of food or drink?"

"Yes," said the Raccoon. "But it is just possible that by this time the green-corn-dumplings may have turned sour."

"I don't care, my dear little brother," said the Wolf, "for I am now starving."

I tried to picture the scene in my mind, but my experience with wolves and raccoons was too limited. I could see only cartoon characters.

So the Raccoon patted his dung between his hands. When he fed the Wolf, he then started off on a walk. After the Raccoon had got some distance on the road, "O Wolf," he said, "it is my dung that you have eaten!"

"What did you say?" said the Wolf. "What is it?"

"It must have been along by this path that our younger brothers passed, is what I said to you," said the Raccoon.

"You disappoint me. A bone he has probably found, thought I in my heart."

A little farther on the road was the Raccoon come when, "O Wolf, it is my dung that you have eaten!"

"What did you say?" said the Wolf.

"It must have been along by this path that our little brothers passed, is what I said to you," said the Raccoon.

"You disappoint me, my dear little brother. Little old dry bones must he have found, thought I in my heart."

Farther along on the road was he going when, "O Wolf, it is my dung that you have eaten!"

"What did you say?" said the Wolf.

"It was perhaps along by this path that our younger brothers passed, is what I said to you," said the Raccoon.

"You disappoint me, my dear younger brother. Little old dry bones he has probably found, thought I in my heart."

A tree not far away was standing, and on it the Raccoon kept his eye as he headed for it. "O Wolf," said he again; "it is my dung that you have eaten!"

"What did you say?" said the Wolf.

"It is my dung that you have eaten!"

"Confound it! rq! rq! rq!" he spit. "Oh, but how will I eat you!"

But the Raccoon hastened up the tree.

As I read the story, I kept thinking of the story James North had told me in the Iowa Memorial Union. The raccoon here is not being as open as that deer had been. The raccoon has not let the wolf enter his body. But the more I thought about it, the more I saw that the raccoon is not being sadistic toward the wolf. In fact, the raccoon gives freely of himself, from the innermost caverns of his past. That is all that he has to give and it is a generous gift — perhaps too generous for the wolf, who does not seem interested in finding his own food.

"Oh, my dear younger brother," said the Wolf; "when do you expect to come down from the tree?"

"When I am so overcome with sleep as to fall," said the Raccoon.

The Wolf then kindled a fire at the foot of the tree. After a little while the Raccoon threw down a piece of bark. "And so now you have fallen!" said the Wolf as he crunched the bark in his mouth. "You deceived me, my dear younger brother," said the Wolf.

Shortly afterward, "Wonder if he is asleep by this time?" thought the Raccoon in his heart. And then another piece of bark he flung down.

"And so now you have fallen!" said the Wolf. And again he crunched the bark in his mouth. "You deceived me, my dear little brother," said the Wolf.

"It was when straightening out my legs that I pushed off the bark with my feet," said the Raccoon. And then a short while after, "Wonder if it is about time for him to be asleep?" thought the Raccoon in his heart. Then he threw down another piece of bark.

Then the Wolf, "And so now you have fallen!" And again he crunched up the bark in his mouth. "You deceived me, my dear little brother," said the Wolf.

"It was when straightening out my legs that I pushed off the bark with my feet," said the Raccoon. Shortly afterward, "Wonder if it is about time for him to be asleep?" thought the Raccoon in his heart. And so he threw down another piece of bark. But the Wolf paid no heed. And then he threw down some more bark. As the Wolf gave no heed, then the Raccoon came down from the tree. Behold, the other was sound asleep! So then he dunged upon the other's eyes. After he was done with dunging upon him, then he left him there.

The wolf did not know the difference between dung and green-corn-dumplings; he does come to know the difference between bark and raccoon. The raccoon is a good teacher.

I had talked to educators in Iowa City and in Tama and had been told that Mesquakie children are considered "motivational problems." When in class with white students, they are extremely quiet and noncompetitive. They seldom ask questions or volunteer answers. I could remember my own elementary school classroom, and I could see students popping their hands into the air excitedly, begging for recognition from the teacher. And I could see the wolf, jumping up from beside the tree and gobbling at the pieces of bark that he hoped might be a raccoon.

When the Wolf awoke from his sleep, his eyes were shut tight with a dried coating. "M, how my eyes must have run with matter, so dry are they caked with it!" He was not able to break the crust apart, and so he started off on a walk. He bumped against a tree and stopped. "Tu! What kind of a tree are you, oh, my dear grandfather?"

"I am an oak."

"How far is it to the river?"

"Why, on the edge of the prairie is where I live."

And then he started off again on the walk. Again he bumped against a tree and stopped. "Tu! What kind of a tree are you, oh, my dear grandfather?"

"I am a walnut."

"How far is it to the river?"

"Oh, a long way off I dwell, my dear grandchild."

And he started off walking again. Once more he bumped against a tree and stopped. "Tu! What kind of a tree are you, my dear grandfather?"

"Why, I am a hickory, my dear grandchild."

"How far is it to the river, my dear grandfather?"

"Why, as a matter of fact some distance away do I live, my dear grandchild."

Again he started off walking. Again he bumped against a tree and stopped. "Tu! What kind of a tree are you, my dear grandfather?"

"Why, I am an elm, my dear grandchild."

"How far is it to the river, my dear grandfather?"

"Why, almost there have you come."

Then he started walking away. He bumped against a tree and stopped. "Tu! What kind of a tree are you, my dear grandfather?"

"I am a hard maple, a stone wood, my dear grandchild."

"How far is it to the river, my dear grandfather?"

"On top of the hill do I stay, and not far away is the river."

Again he started off on a walk. He bumped against a tree and stopped. "Tu! What kind of a tree are you, my dear grandfather?"

"I am a cottonwood, my dear grandchild."

"How far is it to the river, my dear grandfather?"

"Halfway down the hill do I live, my dear grandchild. Not far away is the river."

Again he started off on a walk. He bumped against a tree and stopped. "Tu! What kind of a tree are you, my dear grandfather?"

"I am a sycamore."

"How far is it to the river, my dear grandfather?"

"Only a few more steps and you are there, my dear grandchild."

Then off he started on a walk. He bumped against a tree and stopped. "Tu! What kind of a tree are you, my dear grandfather?"

"I am a willow."

"How far is it to the river, my dear grandfather?"

"Start and take another step, and then you walk into the water, my dear grandchild."

"How deep in the water am I, Wolf that I am?"

"Up to your ankles."

"How deep in the water am I, Wolf that I am?"

"Almost up to your knees."

"How deep in the water am I, Wolf that I am?"

"Up to your knees."

"How deep in the water am I, Wolf that I am?"

"Up to your hips."

"How deep in the water am I, Wolf that I am?"

"Just up to where you fork at the opening."

"How deep in the water am I, Wolf that I am?"

"Up to your navel."

"How deep in the water am I, Wolf that I am?"

"Up to your nipples."

"How deep in the water am I, Wolf that I am?"

"Up to your throat."

"How deep in the water am I, Wolf that I am?"

"Up to your chin."

"How deep in the water am I, Wolf that I am?"

"Up to as far as your mouth."

"How . . . up!" A mink then went down into the water with him.

That is the end of the story.

WOLF THAT I AM ◊ 49

I was beginning to identify with the wolf in this story, just as I saw myself as a raccoon burrowing its way through the intestines of James North's deer. The wolf is, I have been told since, known for his intelligence, yet when he is alone in the woods begging for food and asking questions, he can appear mighty silly.

I suddenly understood why John Waters had changed the subject so suddenly that day outside his house. I had been questioning him too aggressively when he said, "When we Indians have a question or problem, we go to the woods and fast. In that way, an answer can be given to us." He was not volunteering information about religious practices so much as telling me something about the directness of my questions.

Years later, an Indian woman of another tribe told me that it is sometimes considered "bad manners to ask older people too many questions. It is as though you're not showing them proper respect when you're too direct or if you ask too many questions — even in your own family. My father says, 'Be patient and wait until the right time comes and the answer will be given to you.' " The question mark can become a tiny creature that can curl its way right into the heart of another being.

The wolf asked for food and he was given food. The wolf asked for water and he was given his fill. For the seeker of "authentic" information about the Mesquakie Indians, the implication was clear: what is passed off as green-corn-dumplings might well turn out to be dung; and if one wants to see in the water, one had first better learn to swim.

◇ **8** ◇

Wʜᴇɴ I ᴡᴇɴᴛ to the Mesquakie settlement that weekend to talk to Henry Sturgeon, I went alone. The tape recorder was tucked away under the back seat — just in case — but I knew better than to bring it out prematurely. Even if I had had little success in collecting stories, I felt that I had learned a great deal about the Mesquakies and I had spent many hours reevaluating my techniques and procedures.

I knew now that people were easily frightened at the mention of stories, thinking immediately either of their most sacred stories or of the little anecdotes made up for outsiders by people like John Buffalo. These were not the stories I wanted. I decided that I should ask not for stories but for oral history — the events of the past as told by the people who had lived them. These were secular stories, legends, and not the sacred stories that must be kept secret.

It was a dark, windy day and even though it was late morning the sun could not be seen. For the entire trip, I worried about how I would explain my project and how I would introduce my tape recorder. I constructed little scenes in my mind, preparing myself for all the possibilities. I knew that I should be less direct in my approach, but I still dreaded those long minutes of silence that I had experienced at the Clouds's house. By the time I arrived at the Sturgeon house, I had several tentative plans mapped out. As it turned out, I needed none of them.

Henry Sturgeon acted as if he had been expecting me.

Without waiting to hear who I was or what I wanted, he strode across the room rapidly and shook hands with me, then walked back to the dining table that occupied one corner of the long living-dining area and motioned for me to sit down opposite him. Almost immediately, he was talking in what sounded like a story. I surmised that he must have heard of my project from his son, John Sturgeon. But I was caught with neither a tape recorder nor a notebook to record his words and I felt extremely uneasy.

"Let me tell you something," Mr. Sturgeon said with a sweeping wave of the hand. "Our people saw many years ahead of time that the white man was coming. Our people heard a roaring in their ears and they saw in a vision that the white man would come and that he would wear a beard, just like yours, and that he would come from across the waters."

Self-consciously, I reached up to stroke my heavy full beard. Mr. Sturgeon nodded but did not stop talking. His hand and arm gestures were very emphatic, and there was a rhythm in his speech that indicated that he was indeed telling a story. The reference to the beard made me wonder if it was one he was making up on the spur of the moment. But I did not think so.

"So four of our people were chosen to travel from an island in the Mississippi River near what is now Dubuque, Iowa, to the East Coast, where they were to meet the white man." I wanted to interrupt, to ask about those four men but I was not given the opportunity. Mr. Sturgeon kept talking.

"At the same time, across the waters, your people saw in a vision that they would meet a friend across the water. That is the way it was. Your people came because they wanted freedom of religion." Now he stopped for a minute and looked directly at me. "But look at what has happened." I was trying desperately to implant on my memory his intonations and phrasing so that I could later record them. I was not prepared for the implied question that he now seemed to be aiming at me.

After a short pause he continued, gesturing with a wide arc of his arm. *"Mine* were there to meet the white man when he landed in the East." He was pointing to his chest but I looked puzzled and he explained for my benefit: "My people," he said, "my people were there. Yes, my grandfathers met them in the East. You don't know about *yours* but *mine* were there." Again, he pointed to his chest.

Now, I had time to talk. "Do you mean that those people who went to the East were your direct ancestors?" I asked. He nodded, smiling.

"Did you say there were four of them?"

"Four or five."

"Do you know their names?" Of course, their names were not that important to me, but I wanted him to go on, to tell me more details and more stories about these men.

But his answer was as direct as my question. "Yes, I have their names. I know them and I have them written down in a book in the back room."

Now, I was really intrigued. I could see in my mind that ancient ledger filled with the stories of Mesquakie history. I wanted to see the manuscript, to read it and copy it. "You have it written down in a book?" I asked, trying hard not to be too direct.

Mr. Sturgeon nodded. "Someday I may show it to you," he said. But now he was ready to talk again and the gestures resumed. "And let me tell you something. When the white man came here, he wanted one thing — freedom of religion. The Indian let him stay. Today, what has happened to yours? There are over one hundred religions. With ours, there is still only one.

"What we want is what you came across the ocean for — freedom of religion. And we will have it. No one will ever take it away from us." He had answered the question he had posed to me a few minutes earlier. My religion had disintegrated into hundreds of sects. I had grown up listening to petty quarrels and differences between Methodists, Presbyterians, and Congregationalists. But Mr. Sturgeon did not understand; they were really all the same. And none of them were very important to me. Mr. Sturgeon had read too many history textbooks; I knew that my people had come to this country for economic reasons, not for religious freedom.

The storytelling was over for the moment. Henry Sturgeon leaned back in his chair and waited for reaction from me. But I could not be sure that he would not start talking again very soon, and I desperately wanted to have the tape recorder ready. It was a difficult subject to bring up, but I felt that I had established sufficient rapport.

"You know I'm really worried about remembering all this correctly. I have a small tape recorder in the car. I wonder if you would mind if I brought it in?"

"Yes," he said.

I was not sure how he meant that. "Do you mean I can use the tape recorder?"

"No."

He was still sitting calmly and I felt sure I had not disturbed our friendly relationship. Yet he clearly did not intend to elaborate on his reasons for not wanting me to use the tape recorder.

I tried to explain more fully. "Actually, it's only for my benefit. I think that you have said some really important things and I would not want to distort them by not remembering them accurately. It's just to help my memory."

He nodded and his immovable expression indicated that my explanation had not been necessary. "That is what your brain is for," he said. "I'm telling this to you in your language. It is not easy for me. It is up to you to spread the word to your people as *you* understand it."

9

Harry Oster agreed that I should not pursue vigorously the issue of the tape recorder. "Obviously, they have strong feelings about it," he said. "Just do the best you can until you find someone who is willing to be taped." His office seemed to bulge with recorded and unrecorded tapes. Some were filed neatly in bookshelves; others were strewn on tables and under chairs. They looked harmless and inert, but in Oster's folklore classes I had heard these tapes reproduce the sounds of a Mississippi or Louisiana blues man. Some of the tapes had been edited and marketed as recordings.

I was still confused as to why the Mesquakies seemed so insistent that I not use a tape recorder. I felt strongly that it was not merely a superstitious distrust for the machines. No one had noticeably complained when Harry Oster had recorded a song and some conversation that first day. The Clouds had a cassette recorder in their house, and Lucille Waters had talked of getting young people to go with tape recorders to preserve the traditions of their elders. Most Mesquakies seemed to agree that a tape recorder can be a handy device for preserving material that might otherwise be lost.

One of my friends suggested that perhaps the Mesquakies were reluctant to have their stories frozen on tape. But Lucille Waters had confirmed what I had read in books: the stories are not to be changed. They are told word for word as they have been told for centuries and there is no room for the free improvisation that occurs in some forms of oral tradition. Surely, the tape would be a good way of insuring that changes and distortions did not creep into the stories, I thought. Then I could hear Henry Sturgeon's firm voice and I knew that this was not so.

After many years, I still cannot explain the Mesquakie feelings about tape recorders, but experiences have helped me reconcile some of the apparent contradictions. I attended one academic conference, along with several Indian and non-Indian scholars, where the entire proceedings were taped with full knowledge of the participants. John Sturgeon was one of the participants and he did not once mention the tape recorder until the start of a session on "Spirituality and the American Indian." Then, he said: "At this point, I want to see all cameras on the floor, all tape recorders shut off. This is a serious matter. If I come around and see one tape recorder playing, I will crush it with my foot." It was a harsh statement from an otherwise gentle man. Obviously, he felt that some words are more powerful and sacred than others.

Several years later, a man from another Indian tribe — a man of some repute as a medicine man — told me of the time he had been invited to appear on a television show along with other Indians. Until he was ready to go on the air, he was not aware that the show was to be video-taped. When he found out, he was extremely angry, but it was too late to back out of his scheduled appearance.

"Do you know," he said, "when they played back that video tape, everyone else was on it. But nothing I did or said was recorded. It was as if I was invisible and when it was time for me to talk, there was only silence."

My rational mind, trained by years of schooling, refused to accept the literal truth of his story; as a result, I could not share with him an experience that was for him important and real. However, I did understand the implication. The tape recorder is a very practical instrument for recording dead words.

10

Henry and Isabel Sturgeon live on top of a hill, one of the highest parts of the settlement. Just a few yards beyond their house the dirt road becomes paved and the timber of the settlement merges into cultivated Iowa farmland. Their house is a white bungalow, rather large by Mesquakie standards and similar to many houses built in American cities during the 1940s. Set back about fifty yards from the road, the house is surrounded by trees and is always covered by a heavy shade. There are usually one or more spotted ponies grazing near the house, and about fifty yards to the rear the shaded clearing becomes a thick timber.

When I turned into the Sturgeons' drive for my second visit, I saw a young man, apparently in his late teens, standing alone back near the heavy timber. He was wearing a khaki World War I hat, and nestled in his arms, pointing upward at a forty-five-degree angle, was a double-barreled shotgun. He stood without moving and watched me as I stepped out of my car and walked toward the door of the house, dogs snarling at my heels all the way. I felt in imminent danger and persistently fought off a desire to break into a run for safety. But the young man did not move and the dogs did not bite. I was soon safe inside the house.

That image lingered in my mind, but it was so counter to the warm reception that I received at the Sturgeon home that I soon came to doubt its reality. Henry Sturgeon had an uncanny way of understanding me — to the extent that I often wondered if I had met him previously. And even though he was sometimes firm with me, as he had been with the tape recorder, he always managed to remain warm and benevolent.

When I explained more fully my project and told him that Lucy Waters had suggested that he might be of help to me, he reprimanded me subtly. "Lucy Waters? Lucy Waters? I don't know any Lucy Waters. Oh, you mean *Mrs*. Lucille Waters." But then he laughed good-naturedly as Mrs. Sturgeon scolded him: "You knew very well who he was talking about. You call her Lucy too when you're not trying to be superior."

Mr. Sturgeon was seventy-three years of age. His hair was cropped close, with only hints of gray, and his glasses seemed to sit precariously on his high cheekbones.

Very quickly, I felt comfortable around the Sturgeons and the three of us sat around the dining table talking about the upcoming Tribal Council elections. Their son John, who had impressed me so much that first day, was a candidate representing the conservative Old Bear faction. For many years, as they explained, the Old Bear faction had refused to recognize the legitimacy of this governing body, which had been imposed on the tribe by the United States government. The Old Bears had boycotted tribal elections, but in recent years they had come to realize that their interests would not be upheld if they did not vote and run candidates.

Mrs. Sturgeon was herself a former member of the Tribal Council and she talked knowledgeably of tribal politics. She was a thin woman, somewhat tired but serious and intent in her expression. This election was important for her; a victory for her son might help bring about the bilingual, bicultural school for which she had worked so many years.

Mr. Sturgeon was not so concerned about politics. Yes, he nodded, it would be nice if John won the election. "But I have told John," he said, "there is a better way. Nothing is ever solved by politics. The best way is the religious way. If you can keep your religion and worship as you see fit, then the problems will take care of themselves."

Then he shifted his position and looked into my eyes as he told me again about the desires of my ancestors for religious freedom. "Between my religion and yours," he said, "the difference is less than an eyelash." He stopped and repeated himself for emphasis. "Less than an eyelash. But that is in theory. In the Bible, it says that on the fourth day, Christ arose from the dead . . ."

I had to interrupt. "Isn't it the third day?"

"Three or four," he said with a smile. But he didn't continue his argument. It was as if he had already made his point, but I was not sure what it was.

I was unconvinced about the similarity of our religions, and I was particularly unconvinced about the ultimate religious goals of my people. Wasn't it that same kind of naive reliance on religion that had led the American Indian to be exploited by the secular white man?

Now Mr. Sturgeon was talking about the Mesquakie tradition of hospitality. "My house is always open," he said. "The door is never locked and everyone knows that." It would not be wise, I thought, to spread the word too far. "In the old days, they always kept a pot, high off the fire so it would stay warm but not burn, and people knew that they could always come into the lodge and get warm and fill their bellies if they were hungry — other Mesquakies or people from other tribes or other white people. The door was always open. And it is the same today. My door is always open and there is always food in the refrigerator for anyone who is hungry and wants to eat." As Henry Sturgeon was swinging his arm in a friendly arc, the young man with the World War I hat and the shotgun strode through the room without speaking and entered a back bedroom. Mr. Sturgeon motioned to him and said, "That is my younger son — John's brother." I had forgotten about the young man, but now I was once more frightened. He was apparently a hunter, but to me he looked like a warrior.

Mr. Sturgeon continued to talk of hospitality and did not seem to notice anything unusual in his son's appearance. While he had been calmly talking to me about the value of religion and the old way, his son had been out there in the clearing, his shotgun held at a forty-five-degree angle to the sky. My oversimplified notions about "peace pipes" and "war bonnets" were obviously inadequate to help me deal with this seeming contradiction. Mr. Sturgeon continued to talk. He apparently did not see a contradiction.

11

In the weeks that followed, Henry and Isabel Sturgeon recited for me the events of recent Mesquakie history. In fact, they overwhelmed me with history, for I was not yet ready to hear it. They did not give a chronological account of the past and, without a recording device or notebook, I found it very difficult to follow what they were saying. They told stories that seemed to me partial and incomplete, and they made personal references that were to me cryptic. "Some people say, 'What about eighteen ninety-six?'" said Henry Sturgeon. "But I say, 'What about eighteen fifty-four?'" He looked at me as if I should understand what he meant, as if I knew as well as he did these dates and the stories that went with them. The Sturgeons referred again and again to certain dates — 1804, 1832, 1845, 1854, and 1896. These dates recalled for them important events with powerful emotional associations. But without full knowledge of these years, I was lost.

Back in Iowa City, I scurried to historical documents to attempt to fill in the missing elements. The dates, for me, became anchors around which I tried to build a chronological account that could serve as history. In 1804, I discovered, a treaty was made in which the Mesquakies and their allies, the Sacs, were said to give up their claim to lands in Illinois, Missouri, and Wisconsin. The person who signed away this land, under duress, was merely the nominal leader of a small band of Missouri River Sacs. He did not have the authority to make decisions of such far-reaching significance for all of the Mesquakies and Sacs. Most people did not even know of the treaty until they were told that they must leave their home in Illinois and move across the Mississippi River to Iowa.

Reluctantly, the Mesquakies agreed to go and with them went a group of Sacs under Keokuk, a prominent man who had become friendly with the whites. But Black Hawk, a Sac war chief, gathered together a group of young militants who refused to leave. That was in 1832, the beginning of the Black Hawk War.

On an individual basis, some Mesquakies joined Black Hawk's group, as did members of other tribes. As a tribe, the Mesquakies were neutral, but when the war was over, land was taken from both tribes in retribution.

In the years that followed, the United States government recognized Keokuk as the official "chief" of the combined Mesquakie-Sac (or Sac and Fox) tribe. Hereditary leaders of both tribes protested vigorously but to no avail. Under Keokuk's leadership, the remaining land in Iowa was gradually sold to the United States, and finally, in 1845, government troops removed the two tribes, by foot and horseback, from the vicinity of Marengo, Iowa, to a government reservation in Kansas. As the Sturgeons told me, many people refused to make the trip, hiding out along the river banks and in the woods, moving stealthily to keep out of reach of the militia.

Those who accepted the government edict were quickly disillusioned with life in Kansas. There, the corn did not grow and the children got sick and died. Many people were homesick for the old land. A few years before their forced removal, an epidemic had taken the lives of a number of Mesquakie children. These children were buried along the Iowa River and the mothers longed to return and be near their children. When the government tried to force the combined tribes to accept individual rather than communal ownership of the land, there was a political reason to return. Ponies and possessions were sold and a delegation was chosen to go back to Iowa and purchase from white settlers eighty acres of land along the Iowa River.

The good will of white settlers and of the governor of Iowa was obtained. When details were finally arranged, runners were sent to camps all over Iowa to tell those who had refused to go to Kansas that they could now return to their people. The People of the Red Earth, once fragmented, were again integrated. Only through the land could there be unity and harmony, for in the land existed all the spirits of the past, present, and future. In the land was their creation and their destiny.

That was the beginning of the present settlement and I could understand the strong feelings that accompanied these events. For me, it was a sequence of events to be arranged in chronological order and analyzed for causation and meaning. For the Sturgeons, these events were stories which involved their ancestors. Henry Sturgeon's ancestors were in Iowa in 1854 and that meant that he too was part of that creation.

All of these dates and places, the Sturgeons knew with a precision that would embarrass many academic historians, yet their narratives were closer to poetry in richness of expression. "Our people saw many years before that we were to live here — right in the center of the island," said Mrs. Sturgeon with an emphatic gesture toward the ground. I believed that poetry was beautiful and I had devoted my career to its study, but I did not really believe that it could provide literal and factual truth. For my benefit, she added: "That means in Iowa, in the center of the continent that is North America."

I soon came to realize that these accounts of the Sturgeons were neither history nor poetry but prophecy. As they recited the events of the past, they always included reference to the visions of the future. "Our people saw many years before that these events that happened between eighteen thirty-two and eighteen forty-five would take place," said Mrs. Sturgeon. It was the same kind of expression that had been used in the story of the Man with a Beard and I heard it again and again. A woman in Chicago told me that her grandfather, a Winnebago, had been told essentially the same: "Our people saw in a vision many years before that a man named Thunder Cloud would come to visit us and that he would become a friend." Soon, I began to see that this expression was not a cliché but a vision of history. The events of the present and of the future are the visions of a time long past. History is not the linear recounting of dead moments but a re-creation of a meaning that is part of the present — a present that always has been and always will be.

In listening to history told orally, I was learning a definition of history that was different from what I had been taught. I knew of course that history can teach us to avoid the mistakes of the past; however, I was learning that history can teach a great deal more than that. Especially when told orally, history can allow us to live and relive basic experiences — just as the Raccoon's "history" had helped the Wolf find his way to the river.

History brought the Sturgeons closer to their ancestors and to those things that united them as a people. I began to wonder if it could do the same for me. Ironically, my great-great-grandfather had come from Scotland to settle in Illinois in 1854, the same year that the Mesquakies returned to Iowa. What was magic about the year 1854?

One part of me said that the magic was easy to explain. By 1854, all but a small band of renegade Indians had been herded safely away to Kansas and beyond. Large areas of rich farmland were available at bargain prices. My great-great-grandfather had come from a tiny islet in the Atlantic where land is extremely limited. It must have come as an astounding revelation when he discovered that he could lay claim to almost limitless acres of rich, black soil. My great-great-grandfather had come to this country for economic reasons.

But I had been to visit that tiny island, the Isle of Bute, and I had stood on a gentle green hillside looking out over the water. I remembered what Yeats said about the ability of the sea to inspire awe and I remembered the many voyage stories of Celtic mythology. There was The Voyage of Bran and the story of Brendan the Navigator, who is said to have sailed west to discover the "Happy Isles" many years before Christopher Columbus. That story had always intrigued me, and I had named my second son Brendan after that mythical character.

Saint Brendan had traveled west in search of the East and so had Christopher Columbus. Part of me wanted to believe that my great-great-grandfather had been drawn by the same magical lure to cross the water in 1854. If that were true, then Mr. Sturgeon was right: my people had seen in a vision many years before that they would cross the water and find a new land. They had come for religious reasons. They had traveled to the West in search of renewal, rebirth. They were hunters in the Indian sense of the word.

If I could believe that story, then my beard was no accident. I was, in 1971, both the first and the last white man to visit the Mesquakie settlement. But Mr. Sturgeon had warned me that my ancestors had lost sight of their original purpose — they had traveled 100 roads and had failed to find the meaning and purpose that they sought. They had failed to accept the vision of the West — a vision of one road and one meaning.

If that was the story, then I had to study carefully my goals. If I was indeed guided by a vision, then I must not let that vision become obscured by the material values of my culture.

I wanted to believe Henry Sturgeon's story; I wanted to believe his vision of history. But was it myth or history? I was not sure.

12

W<small>HEN</small> H<small>ENRY</small> S<small>TURGEON</small> had told me about the four Mesquakies who were sent to meet the Man with a Beard on the eastern coast of the island, he said that their names were written in a book that he kept in the back room of his house. On my second visit, he mentioned the book again. "Do you remember that book I told you about?" he asked. He was leaning back in his chair, smiling, and I suspected that he might be teasing. But I was extremely anxious to see that book and I did not succeed in concealing my eagerness. In my imagination, I could see that ancient ledger full of historical material that no white man had ever seen. The script would be difficult to read, but in it would be innumerable secrets. If I could only see it, I would be able to make an outstanding contribution to American Indian scholarship — of that I was sure.

Mr. Sturgeon was sitting silently, his arms at his side, looking at me. We were alone in the room, but the television set was on and the quizmaster was shouting irrelevant comments. "Do you think I could see the book?" I asked.

"Someday on one of your visits, I might bring it out and show it to you," he said. He laughed as he arose from his chair and walked into the kitchen. He returned with two pears and offered me one to eat. "It's lunchtime," he said. "Have a pear." The skin was rough, but the meat inside was cool and sweet. He talked no more of the ancient book.

During the following week, I grew more and more impatient to see that ledger. When I visited him on Friday, I mentioned it again, and again he told me that some day, on one of my visits, he might show it to me. He seemed to be deliberately teasing me, whetting my appetite for something that might not even exist. But my frustration continued to build and I looked forward to each meeting with increased excitement.

On the fourth week, I intended to remain quiet, to let him bring up the subject of the book. Again, we were alone, with the television set blaring loudly in the background. Outside, the wind was blowing in heavy gusts, rattling the windowpanes. Mr. Sturgeon talked slowly and quietly, but I could not listen for my mind was on the book that I had not yet seen. Finally, I decided that I could wait no longer. Obliquely but awkwardly, I worked mention of the book into the conversation.

This time, Mr. Sturgeon was not so patient with me. He laughed and rose from his chair to walk across the room. "Ho! So you want to see those names?" He was not angry but noticeably irritated. "Why do you need to know that? Why, my own daughter does not know that. Why do you think you need to know that?" Then he sat down and the ledger was never mentioned again.

◇ **13** ◇

THE WARM FALL WEATHER had been an illusion. The leaves were by now off the trees and raked away, leaving the earth naked and exposed to the cold winds. We had ordered a load of coal for the basement of our antiquated farmhouse and were spending more and more time inside.

By now I was traveling at least three days every week to the Mesquakie settlement, and the trips were becoming more and more a part of my daily life. Duncan and Brendan still wanted to hear "stories" from my visits. I told them of the Raccoon and the Wolf, a story that still haunted me, and I told them of my experiences driving down the roads of the Mesquakie settlement. They knew the place and they were happy with my stories, even if I was not.

Donna, an Australian by birth and a graduate student of medieval French literature, had no external reason to be interested in the oral literature of an American Indian people, but she had become as involved as I was in the process that was taking place. We talked constantly of the Mesquakies, of their history and of their current problems with the school. She knew the people and the stories as well as I did and we shared insights.

In the library we were together and, as often as her work allowed her, she accompanied me to the settlement. I no longer needed her company to protect me against the threatening silences. We were both learning that silence can be an important means of communication — a way of stripping bare the empty phrases and phony rituals that sometimes creep into conversations. But it was important for her to be with me. I no longer felt torn between my work and my family, and the Sturgeons seemed to enjoy talking to the two of us. For some occasions, such as the interchanges involving the ancient book, Henry Sturgeon seemed to wait until he could relate to me on a one-to-one basis. But it was on occasions when the four of us were together that anecdotes and pieces of history were most likely to be told.

It was a cold, windy day, damp and dark, when Donna and I made a Friday afternoon visit with the Sturgeons. The first snowfall, which had been imminent for several weeks, had not yet come. As we arrived, Mr. Sturgeon was still seated at the table, leaning back in his chair. On a platter before him were huge, tantalizing chunks of meat that appeared to be neither beef nor pork. Perhaps venison? The smell of food was powerful. Mrs. Sturgeon and her teen-aged daughter were hastily clearing the table, preparing for a trip to Marshalltown.

Mr. Sturgeon leaned his chair back on its hind legs and looked at us from across the room. We were seated on the sofa on the far side of the long room. Between us, the TV set was blurting out the midday news. We talked about the cold weather but Mr. Sturgeon was not interested in discussing the weather. "Do you think I can tell you if it is going to snow?" he said with a short laugh.

Then very suddenly, he changed the subject. "So what can I do for you today?" he asked. The question surprised me in its directness and I fought off the urge to bring up yet again the old book in the back room.

"I don't know," I said. "I'd just like to talk. Whatever you feel like talking about."

A long silence, then Mr. Sturgeon said, "You're interested in stories, aren't you?" Then another silence, as I nodded.

He arose from the table as if the subject had been disposed of. He was of medium build with broad shoulders and large hands. He was slightly stooped and his limp was noticeable as he moved into the living room and sat down opposite us in an overstuffed chair. I'm not sure I succeeded in hiding my impatience to hear stories. He was smiling at me as he had earlier when he had brought up the ancient ledger.

He teased me about my beard. "What do you think about that?" he asked Donna. But he didn't wait for an answer. "You know, *we* don't grow beards," he said. "Indians don't grow beards." His eyes blinked at us sleepily through his dark-rimmed spectacles. He did not seem to be joking any longer.

"That's right," he continued. "We never start shaving and so we never grow beards and we never have to shave." As a teenager I had believed it — shaving made the beard grow faster and longer. Many times I had shaved secretly, gliding the razor over my smooth face, hoping to create the beard that would change me from a boy to a man. My parents knew, and they laughed at my naiveté.

Mr. Sturgeon was looking intently at me through his glasses. He knew that I was doubtful and wary of being teased again. "You don't believe me, do you?" Then he looked at Donna for confirmation. She smiled but refused to commit herself. He went on in earnest. "It's true. I've seen Indians who went all their lives without shaving. Then they started shaving and they grew a beard — just like that. It's true."

Mr. Sturgeon's head was round and his gray hair was clipped short along the temples. There was a certain way he held his head, a certain stiffness on one side of the neck, that reminded me of my father. The more he talked, the more I realized the similarity — the glasses, the expression, the voice. But I'm sure that no one else would have seen any similarity.

I did not know now if he was playing a joke on me. His expression was serious and he seemed truly concerned that we were not accepting his assertions. "You know, it happened to my son John. You know John. He went into the navy during the war, and they were determined to make him shave. So he wrote home and said, 'What am I going to do, Dad. They say I have to shave. And I know that once I start shaving, then I'll have to keep it up for the rest of my life.'"

"Really?"

"It's true."

"So what did he do?"

"He started shaving — they made him. And now he has to shave." The story was becoming too convincing to ignore. We were indignant toward the insensitive naval officer.

Mr. Sturgeon was looking at us intently. "I have never shaved in my life," he said. "And I don't have a beard."

"Really?"

"That's right. Look at my face. I have never shaved and you can see that I don't have a beard." It was obviously true; his face was smooth and unbearded. My scientific belief was being undermined. I could tell that Donna was struggling with the same doubts. I could remember looking at myself in the mirror, carving slowly around my chin while my father smiled at me in the mirror. "So you think that you'll make it grow faster." He laughed.

Mr. Sturgeon was shifting his gaze from me to Donna and back again. He was getting the assurance he was seeking and he leaned back in his overstuffed chair. As he talked, his fingers played with a small metallic object and his hands moved repeatedly from his face to the arm of the chair. Only then did I begin to notice his movements.

He leaned forward in his chair for emphasis. "Actually, when I want to get rid of hair on my face, I can do it any time. I don't need a mirror or a razor." He held up what appeared to be a tiny coil or spring. Then he moved it back to his face. "This is my razor," he said. "When I am at work or anywhere else, all I have to do is . . ." And he demonstrated by plucking whiskers with the tiny coil.

The three of us laughed. I felt that my beard had grown immeasurably in the few moments it had taken him to tell the story. Mr. Sturgeon did indeed remind me of my father.

◊ 14 ◊

As we were driving back to Iowa City, the first snowflakes of winter began to fall. When I returned alone the following Friday at my regular time to see Mr. Sturgeon, the ground was covered with a thick blanket of white. As I shook the snow from my boots, Mr. Sturgeon greeted me from his place at the dining table. He was alone and sitting almost exactly as he had been the week before when I had arrived. The platter of meat was gone, but the smell of food was overwhelming. I could reconstruct the scene that had taken place a few minutes before.

He did not move from his place and I walked over to the table to sit opposite him. Just as he had a week earlier, Mr. Sturgeon leaned back in his chair, smiled serenely, and asked: "What can I do for you today? What is it you want to know?"

I still did not know how to respond. I did not want to be too pushy, yet this seemed to be an invitation. I was noncommittal. "Nothing in particular. Anything you feel like talking about."

Mr. Sturgeon laughed. "So you say you want to learn about stories? Well, I don't know as much as some people. My grandfather told me most of what I know, but it has always seemed that they were incomplete, that something was missing. He died when he was only about fifty, and I've always wondered if that didn't have something to do with it."

I respected Mr. Sturgeon's silence for several minutes before I responded. "What I'd like to do is get a group of people together for a storytelling session. I'd just like to be there and see what goes on between the storyteller and the audience. That would seem to be the best way to learn about stories, don't you think?"

"I don't know. Maybe it would."

"Do you think I could do that?"

"No." A long silence. "My son John has been trying to do that very thing for quite a while. It's a matter of getting people to agree to come together for that purpose. And if John couldn't succeed in getting people together, I don't think you would have much luck."

"Don't people tell the stories anymore?"

He shook his head emphatically. "People still tell stories."

"Are there certain people known as storytellers?"

"No. Some people know some things and other people know other things. No one person knows all the stories and anyone can tell stories." As he paused, he looked up at the ceiling as if he could see pictures or words there. He was ready to talk.

"In the old days, as I learned from my grandmother on my mother's side, people would gather, once the snow had fallen, in a warm wickiup around the fire. And the people would sit in a circle around the fire and tell stories. Sometimes one person would tell stories and sometimes several people would tell stories. But the signal to begin telling stories would be when the person was given some tobacco." I did not smoke, but I felt that I should have brought some cigarettes with me. "And he would smoke the pipe and tell stories. It was very important while the story was being told that everyone give absolute attention to the storyteller. There could be no talking and no interruptions. Discipline was one of the things to learn from the story. You were to learn how to be patient and listen to stories. And if you sat down with crossed legs you would stay that way until the end of the story." I stiffened in my chair and tried to remain still. It was incredibly difficult to maintain that kind of discipline.

Mr. Sturgeon continued: "You listened and at the end there was a break and you could get up and walk around or you could ask questions. Then another story would be told and stories would continue to be told until people had fallen asleep. And at that time the man who had been telling stories would shout out: 'Is there anyone here to listen to stories?' And if no one answered, then the storytelling would be over for that night."

Mr. Sturgeon was talking to me, in a language I could understand, about things his grandmother had told him many years before — perhaps around a wickiup fire. We were sitting in a white bungalow at the top of a hill.

Mr. Sturgeon continued: "When someone has stories or knowledge that you would like to learn, you can invite that person, who is more likely an older person, a man or a woman, over to your house to tell stories." He was now talking about a more recent event — a continuing tradition. "You would tell that person what you wanted and you would invite him or her over to your house. And he might decide to come or he might not come. It is up to him. But you would give him some tobacco and that would be the signal that he was to start telling stories. This would usually take place at night when he was relaxed and you would sit in the living room. And it is important to listen carefully. If you were sitting in one position when the story started, you were to be sitting in that same position when it ended. The discipline of listening to stories is something to be learned. Then after the story was over, you could ask questions, but not until the story was over."

I got the clear impression that Mr. Sturgeon's repetition was not a lapse of memory. He was not repeating a fact but reenacting an action — once in a wickiup and once in a white bungalow. There was at the moment a lamp beside his head and I could envision smoke rising from a pipe and curling toward the ceiling, trying to escape through a smokehole.

"When something happens that seems impossible, you are supposed to ask yourself, 'How can that be?' And by asking the question, you can learn more from the story. The mixture of the possible with the impossible makes us ask questions and helps us learn more.

"And, if you wanted, you could ask a second person, rather than the storyteller, a question about the story. But if you did, you had to remember that these two people could get together before the next story was told. And say, for example, there were two people who asked questions of another person. And the storyteller might say, 'There are two here who do not believe my story.' And that would be to let those two people know that he knew that they had asked someone else about his story."

I remembered, with a start, that when Donna and I had left the Sturgeons' house the week before, we had stopped for a few minutes to talk with another older Mesquakie, a man who was in the opposite political faction and definitely not a friend of Henry Sturgeon's. We had asked this man questions about Mesquakie customs concerning shaving. Mr. Sturgeon seemed to know of our visit but I did not know how. I blushed to think that he knew so much about me.

He was still speaking: "And it would be best if they had asked the storyteller the question first, just as a child might come to his parents to ask if he can visit someone else's house." He held his head to the side.

"And when a storytelling session is over, the people are to get up without touching their hands to the floor."

A long silence, then Mr. Sturgeon again looked to the ceiling as if he were going way back — back beyond the time when stories were first told around a wickiup fire. Then he looked at me and continued: "You know *you* have a story about the Turtle and the Hare." It was, of course, a story about patience. "Well, we have a story that is like it." Then he began:

There was this great big lake. And there was a Turtle. And I cannot remember whether it was a Deer or a Rabbit. But anyway this race was planned.

And the Turtle got together ahead of time with other turtle friends and set them up in certain key places along the line of the track. He set up these other turtles. And when the race started, the Deer was running on the ground and the Turtle was in the water. And every time the Deer would come to one of these selected places, one of the Turtle's friends would lift up his head. And the Deer would say, "Oh, I am losing this race." And then he would run faster. And he would come to the next place and there ahead of him a Turtle would pop up his head. And the Deer would think, "I am losing this race." And he would run even faster. And at every step along the line, one of the Turtle's friends would lift up his head and the Deer would run even faster because he thought that he had lost the race.

And at the end of the line, the first and the last Turtle popped up his head and won the race. The first and the last Turtle was the Turtle that was racing him and he was there all the time and didn't move but had just had his friends scattered around the water on the outside edge.

The story was over and the tension relaxed. I shifted my position and crossed and recrossed my legs. The story seemed too simple for what I had expected. It was another version of the Tortoise and the Hare, but I did not know what questions I should ask the storyteller.

Mr. Sturgeon was looking directly at me. His shoulders were somewhat stooped and his neck curved out awkwardly from his body. He seemed to know what I was thinking. Since I didn't have any questions, he asked one of me:

"If no one had any questions, the storyteller might ask, 'What would be the difference if the Turtle were racing on the ground and the Deer in the water?'" He waited a while, but it was apparent that I did not have the answer. He continued, "And the answer would be, 'There is no difference since the

Deer would not know his way through all the hidden holes of the water.' "

"You mean the Turtle would win that race too — even if he were on the ground and the Deer were in the water?"

Mr. Sturgeon nodded. Now I was puzzled. It was, after all, the cover of the water that gave the Turtle its advantage.

"But isn't the Deer a good swimmer?"

Mr. Sturgeon looked directly at me and nodded.

Then I frantically began to ask questions. But they got me nowhere.

"Is the Turtle always a trickster?"

"Always."

"Isn't the Raccoon also a trickster?"

"Yes. And there are other tricksters."

"Does the water have anything to do with the Turtle's power as a trickster?"

"Yes."

Mr. Sturgeon continued to look at me with a knowing smile, but my questions failed to elicit any further response from him. The story was over. He had told it to me in my language — that was not easy for him and he had teased me for many weeks before deciding if he should do so.

Shortly after, Mrs. Sturgeon came home from a trip to Marshalltown and Mr. Sturgeon did not want to talk further about the story. He was through telling stories for the day; perhaps he had given me all that he was prepared to give.

As I drove back and forth between Iowa City and Tama, I thought about the story many times. But it was nearly a year before I thought of the questions that I should have asked Mr. Sturgeon. By then, of course, the answers were mine.

When I returned to Iowa City, my first impulse was to look up the story Mr. Sturgeon had told me in the published collections of Jones and Michelson. I still distrusted my own memory, my ability to hear the story and get it right. I needed something tangible — a text on the page in front of me to study, or a tape to listen to again and again — to help me understand the story.

But I did not find the text that I wanted, and I was left with only my memory, faulty though I feared it to be, of Mr. Sturgeon telling the story to me. I could clearly see him sitting in the easy chair, his neck held out awkwardly from his rounded shoulders, his eyes blinking sleepily behind his black-rimmed glasses. And I could feel my own discomfort — sitting stiffly and awkwardly on the couch, fighting off the impulse to scratch my nose or recross my legs, trying hard to remember every word. When I thought about the story in the weeks that followed, that experience of hearing it was always first to surface, overwhelming my attempts to remember and understand the details.

I could not be sure that I remembered the text of the story correctly or that it was an authentic version. I had wanted to observe a story being told, in Mesquakie, to a Mesquakie audience, but Mr. Sturgeon told me that was impossible. Instead, I had to be satisfied with a story, in English, told to me, with only my unreliable memory to record it. I was not at all sure that this story would be acceptable as folklore scholarship. But at the same time I knew that it was the most I could expect from Mr. Sturgeon or any other Mesquakie.

I thought about the story for many months, and I tried to reconstruct it as a bedtime story for Duncan and Brendan. And when I relaxed in bed at night, I could feel myself being told the story by Henry Sturgeon. I could see his round face and hear his nasal, hesitant voice; and sometimes when I relaxed enough, the storyteller became my father, and he was telling me something very clear and very simple. But when I awoke and tried to write down what he was telling me, it vanished — like a summer breeze blowing through the tree outside my bedroom window.

When I was awake, I theorized. I was the Deer and Mr. Sturgeon was the Turtle; I was linear and he was cyclical. But that kind of thinking was itself linear and a part of the Western academic structure. I had been trained to see dichotomies, distinctions, differences. I did not know how to live in a white frame house with a wickiup beside it or a white bungalow with indoor plumbing that could, in the imagination, become a wickiup with a fire and a smoke hole.

James North once told me that "a story is something that really happened and when I hear a story, I believe it." As much as I wanted to, I did not believe Mr. Sturgeon's story.

When I was ten years old, I had a pet turtle. I found it in the road beside our house and I took it home and kept it in a galvanized tub out by the barn. It was a good-sized turtle, about as big as a large saucer, with a humped shell that was green with yellow stripes. My older brother told me that turtles live to a very old age — maybe several thousand years — and that they grow very slowly until they become so big that men can ride them like horses. I had seen the little turtles with painted shells that were sold at the state fair; at the zoo I had seen turtles big enough to ride. Judging by its size, I figured that my turtle must be at least several hundred years old.

I spent a lot of time with my turtle. I liked to watch him crawl slowly along, thumping his shell against the concrete of the driveway. And I would place him on his back and watch him deftly stick out his long neck, form a pivot against the ground, and very quickly flip his shell over upright. It took him only a few seconds to accomplish this and I could tell that his neck muscles were very strong. When poked out of the shell, his head and neck looked dangerously like a snake. At times I was not thinking I would become frightened when he stretched his neck and blinked his eyes at me.

My turtle's eyes were very strange. The lids were very thin, almost transparent, and they closed from the bottom up. When he swam in the tub, he would pull up his eyelids, but I could see his eyes through the transparent covering. And sometimes he would stay under the water for hours, staring out through his transparent eyelids. Since his eyes were on opposite sides of his head, he could not focus on one location as I could. I wondered if he saw one image or two, or merely one continuous panorama — like a picture taken with a fisheye lens.

I never did discover for sure whether it was a land or a water turtle. When I filled the tub with dirt, he seemed happy. And when I filled it with water, he seemed equally happy. Finally, I compromised by putting a large stone in the middle of the tub, surrounded by several inches of water. The rock itself was shaped somewhat like an upside-down turtle, and when the turtle rested on the stone, it looked as if there were two turtles, bottom to bottom — or perhaps a reflection of one turtle in the water.

My biggest problem was finding food for my turtle. I gave him lettuce, grass, meat scraps; I even killed flies and put them in his tub. But I never saw him eat. I was afraid that he was fasting to protest his captivity, but I could not bring myself to give him his freedom. And when I tried to force food into his mouth, he merely drew his head into his shell. Perhaps, I thought, turtles eat very little or maybe nothing. But how could I be sure? If he had been a dog, I could have seen him getting thinner. But how could I possibly tell if my turtle was undernourished?

I kept my turtle in his tub and tended him regularly through most of the summer and fall, but when cold weather came, my visits to his tub became less frequent. Finally, one snowy day while I was indoors playing, my brother came rushing inside carrying my turtle. He was shouting at me: "Look at what you've done. You've let your turtle freeze to death." Ice and snow were packed tightly into the crevices where the turtle hid his head, legs, and tail.

I cried for hours as I thought of the cruel death I had inflicted on a creature by refusing to give him the freedom he so clearly desired. Finally, I placed the lifeless shell on the floor beside the stove. I would have to wait for a warmer day to give it a proper burial.

Several hours later, when we were eating supper, there came a sudden loud thumping. It was a very distinct and loud thump as if someone were poking a broom from the underside of the floor. It would stop momentarily, then begin again.

We all got up from our chairs, and at almost the same moment we realized the origin of the thumping. The turtle was walking, slowly but with patient progress, from his place by the kitchen stove toward the dining room table. The ice and snow had melted into a puddle on the floor and my turtle had miraculously come back to life.

That was a story that had really happened; it was so fantastic I could scarcely believe it.

◇ 16 ◇

THE WINDOW in Bob Sayre's office provided a long vertical frame for the bank of the Iowa River. I could see only a small portion of the river, framed on top and bottom by snow. Soon the river would be frozen solid and students would walk across from the men's dormitories on one side to the English-Philosophy Building on the other. The framed view of the river was always exciting, with a massive weeping willow tree in the foreground.

Bob Sayre's head was silhouetted in the window as he leaned back in his chair and listened to my problems. By now, I knew for sure that there was a living oral literature among the Mesquakies. But I did not have the time to do the collecting job that I had planned. At this rate, I would be lucky to hear ten or fifteen stories a year — and then only if I accepted the Mesquakies' terms, which made it extremely difficult to get the fully documented texts that professional folklorists expect.

"I don't think that matters, do you?" Bob Sayre asked.

"No, but I don't know what else I should do."

"What do you think you should do?"

I thought a while and when I answered it was as if I were in a graduate seminar. I was giving a minilecture. "Well, it seems to me that Mesquakies know their stories in a completely different way. I was totally puzzled when Mr. Sturgeon told me that story, yet I could tell that he thought the meaning should be very simple. I'd like to know what goes on in a Mesquakie mind when a story is told. I'd like to know how a Mesquakie goes about interpreting and understanding a story and how this compares to the way we interpret literature."

It had seemed like the right thing to say when I started out, but I knew as soon as I was finished that none of the Mesquakies I knew would tell me what was going on inside his or her head when a story was told. That, of course, was private, like Henry Sturgeon's book.

"How about an interpreting session?" Sayre said, interrupting my reverie with a spur-of-the-moment decision. "I'll invite a couple of my students. You and Donna can come, and you can invite James North to come, if you like. How about tonight at eight o'clock at my house?"

It was a good idea. I needed Bob Sayre's decisiveness to get me going again. I did not think James North would come, but it might be a useful experiment even if he didn't. I know that I needed help in understanding the stories.

James North lived with a roommate in one of the towering men's dormitories across the river. While I had never seen a telephone on the Mesquakie settlement, James did have a phone in his room and he always seemed to answer it almost before it rang.

"Yeah," he said as he picked up the phone. I felt as if I were already in the midst of a conversation.

"James?"

"Yeah, Freddy."

I felt very uncomfortable talking to him on the phone. It was as if he were watching me on a television screen while I could hear only his telephone-muffled voice.

I found myself apologizing too much as I explained about the session, but it didn't matter. "Sure, I'll come," he said. "Can you pick me up at the dorm?"

It was dark when Donna and I pulled up in front. James ran out to the car. He was bundled up tightly in his navy pea jacket which, in the dark, made him look even more bearlike.

James had attended a prestigious liberal arts college in California and he had read his poetry throughout the country. Surely, the environment was as familiar to him as it was to us. We sat in leather-covered chairs in Bob Sayre's book-lined study, drank Burgundy, and ate cheese and potato chips. James sat very near me and was even quieter than usual. When he did speak, it was usually in an undertone and directed only to me and not to the group.

The session quickly became a seminar. I read stories from William Jones's collection and we discussed them. We all looked hopefully and questioningly at James but he seldom responded. He examined the books very carefully, and from time to time he would lean over to point out to me, in a quiet voice, a story or tradition that he recognized. As the rest of us carried on a literary discussion, he listened and watched. Once he told me how to pronounce the name of Wisaka, the person who created the culture of the Mesquakies. "Wee-su-kǎ-hä," he said for me. The last syllable was a voiceless blow from high in the throat and no matter how hard I tried, I could not get it right. James shrugged; the others laughed.

Everyone enjoyed the story of the Raccoon and the Wolf but the discussion did not seem particularly helpful. James was silent, but when we started asking questions about raccoons, he volunteered the story he had told me earlier about the raccoons who had crawled inside the anus of the deer. This time, however, there were five rather than two raccoons in the story and I counted five white faces in the room. "But I'm not sure I remember the story correctly," he said as he finished. "And I really don't know much about raccoons."

I then read the story of the Mouse that had crawled inside the body of the Deer. James nodded but did not comment about the similarity of the story to his. Without him, the discussion quickly bogged down, and I moved on to another story.

Because I was still struggling to understand the story Mr. Sturgeon had told me, I then read a story of "How the Turtle Brought Ruin upon Himself." The story was very long but extremely funny and as I read I could sense that everyone in the room was giving absolute attention and full participation. For a minute, I enjoyed the pleasure that a storyteller must feel when he knows that he has recreated an experience for his audience.

The story relates how the Turtle, once a powerful and important manitou or god, lost his position. It seems the Turtle, always an expert gambler, insulted Wisaka, his gaming partner, because he had mourned so long the death of his younger brother. Wisaka became very angry at the Turtle and vowed revenge. He did so by disguising himself as a beautiful maiden, taking the name little Doe-Fawn, and going to a tiny lodge, a lodge where women go during their menstrual periods. There he was met and fed a very special meal by a very old grandmother.

Wisaka knew that the Turtle had a particular weakness for the women; that was how he planned to trick him. Soon, the Turtle unceremoniously pushed his way into the lodge, insulted the grandmother, and tried to seduce the young woman. The powerful Wisaka exercised his power by being as meek and passive as a little doe-fawn. And naturally the Turtle exploited the situation.

Alone with the maiden, the Turtle started telling stories, but little Doe-Fawn insisted that he fetch his sacred bundle in order that she could believe him. So he got his sacred bundle, desecrating it by taking it into the menstrual lodge, and when his brother protested, the Turtle insulted his brother, just as he had insulted his former friend Wisaka.

So they made for themselves a place to lie down. Then after a little while the Turtle began to swell with an erection of the penis. "Let us put something under our heads for a pillow," said the woman. So they lay with a pillow under their heads; the sacred bundle was the pillow. Now was the time when the Turtle let his hand steal softly over her to find how big she was at the vulva. And then he went in unto her. It was hard work before he could make her possible; yet it was pleasant after he was done with her. She tickled him in the loins and would not let up until he went in unto her again. And when they were done he said to her: "I say, let us rest! Do, for a short while, little Doe-Fawn! Let us spin away at some yarns."

"I really am never in the habit of doing any such thing as that, so I have nothing to tell about. Now this thing which we are doing is surely more delightful. What good is to come from the spinning of tales, anyhow!"

"Ah, it is true that there is more pleasure in this kind of thing." And so he went in unto her again. By this time he was thoroughly tired out. After a while he was done with lying with her. And as they lay there together, he was bent on telling stories; but whenever he began a tale, she would close his mouth with her hand. At last she said to him: "What do you want with the stories? (If you could not keep up this thing), then you had no business to get me started in the first place."

"I say, let me alone for a little while. Do wait, then by and by it will be again."

"Pray, what is the matter with you? I wish to speak the truth, was what you certainly said a while ago. Now there is no sense whatever to be merely lying here all the time.

"Why, don't you take any delight at all in it? As for me, I am quite pleased with it." So he went in unto her again, this time he was a long while at it. She teased him more than ever, and he really had a hard time getting done. "Now, then, let us go to sleep, Doe-Fawn."

She tickled him in the loins and would not let him rest. But at last the Turtle fell asleep. She shook him hard, but he did not wake. Then the woman made ready and rose to her feet. She went in search of a log fallen to decay, and found one alive with ants. She brought it and placed it where he lay. The

Turtle slept with it, and it crumbled when he took hold of it with the hand. Then, taking up the sacred bundle, she went away.

As for the Turtle, he was fast asleep. Something kept waking him, and he would always say: "Oh, be quiet, little Doe-Fawn!" After a while he grew wide awake. Wishing to pass his hand gently over the girl, he began to feel, and the touch of the body was strange. Thinking in his heart that he would look upon her, lo! it was a chunk of wood he was looking at. Behold! the woman was gone, and so was his sacred bundle.

The room was alive with laughter. There was something universally comic about this story that could easily survive translation, even though there were obviously many cultural details that we could not understand fully without being a Mesquakie. The story was not over, but I was laughing too much to continue reading.

One of Sayre's students took the opportunity to ask a question: "What *is* a sacred bundle?" It was not addressed to anyone in particular, but we all instinctively looked at James. He sat silent, looking back at me. Then he replied, quietly: "Go ahead, Freddy."

"Well, I know what the books say," I apologized. I felt extremely uncomfortable playing the role of the academic expert in front of someone who knew the subject firsthand. I looked at James but he would give no help. "They are bundles which contain certain artifacts — say a peace pipe and a flute and a bill of a duck. These things are symbolic of important things that have happened in the past. They are wrapped up in a leather or buckskin bundle and hung on the wall so they will be safe. A certain person in each clan or religious society is in charge of the sacred bundle for that group, and that person has a responsibility to see that the bundle is not abused. When the right time comes, the bundle is used in a religious ceremony. But a sacred bundle is never supposed to touch the ground and, of course, it is not to be treated like this." I looked to Donna to see if there was anything I had forgotten. Then I looked to James North, but he sat there with the same expression. I was sweating heavily. It was as if I myself had been faced with the responsibility of protecting a sacred bundle. I tried to conceal my anxiety and started to read again.

It seems the Turtle searched for Doe-Fawn and his missing sacred bundle for many months. He searched until he was exhausted and it was a long time since he had eaten any food.

So he (the Turtle) went away. Over there as he went traveling along he happened to think of his friend Wisaka. "Now I have it, it is my friend! To him will I go. Surely will my friend not fail to know her. Yes, thither will I go, where he lives. Being a friend of mine, of course he will tell me." In such wise did he feel in his heart. So he went away to the place where (Wisaka) lived. When he was come, he passed inside.

"Welcome!" Wisaka said to him. "You must have been sick," the Turtle was told.

"Not at all, my friend. They have brought ruin upon me."

"Who?"

"A woman. She took my sacred bundle and went away with it. For that reason have I come, that I might ask you if you know of anybody who would go by such a name as Doe-Fawn?"

"Not at all do I know of any one of that name. But I have some pet animals here, and I call them Little Fawns. Yet I do not know how they could cause you harm. Go look at them. They are naughty little creatures."

"Alas, it must have been my friend! He is the one who must have caused my ruin!" Thus he began to feel in his heart. So he went to look at the fawns, and his friend came along as company.

"Well, here they are. Take a look at them."

So he looked at them. Lo! and there was his sacred bundle. It had been trampled and kicked quite into shreds. Only a little bit was left for him to see. Then he began to weep.

(Wisaka) went up to him and took him by the tail. "You stung me with insult at the time when you taunted me about my younger brother."

"Woe is me! Don't, my friend, be too cruel with me!"

"Of course I will not be too cruel with you." Then he gave him a fling, throwing as if to hit a pond. And there was where (the Turtle) landed. In a little while he came to the surface of the water, there above the mossy scum which lay over the water.

"Now that is the way it shall be with you. My uncles and my aunts will often use you for food. But some of them will not eat of you. They will loathe you because of your ugly look. So then, I have nothing more to say to you."

That is the end of the story.

After the laughter calmed down, I read a passage from William Jones's ethnography in which he explained that the story shows that the Turtle retained only one of his former powers — the power of long life. Another ending to the story shows that the medicine of the Turtle is to keep the "breath of life" on this side of the river rather than in the land of death on the other side. Wisaka instructed the Turtle: "When men come to you and ask you for this medicine, tell them where to find it."

Most of those in the room looked puzzled by this explanation. James North looked unimpressed. I had destroyed the mood that the story had created, and I struggled to recapture it by carrying the ribaldry one step further: "It just goes to show that you have to be careful where you put your bundle," I said. There were awkward giggles.

I had for a moment forgotten James North's presence and he was looking at me, trying to get my attention. He spoke very quietly: "I'm afraid I'm going to have to be getting back to the dorm," he said. "I've got some studying to do. Would you mind giving me a ride?"

The others decided to leave too; the party was over. No one had noticed, but I felt strongly that my last remark had been too sacrilegious for James North. My flippant comment was an insult comparable to the insult the Turtle had flung at Wisaka. I had a sinking feeling in the pit of my stomach as I gathered up my books.

In the car, James leaned forward from the back seat and called: "Hey, Freddy! Your headlight on the left side is burned out. I noticed when you picked me up. You've got a one-eyed Ford! Did you know that!"

James sat back, but a moment later he again pulled himself up and leaned on the back of the seat between my head and Donna's. "Hey! You want to hear a song?"

Donna and I listened carefully as he sang, chanting in unknown words, then singing in English:

> After the dance is over
> I will take you home
> In my one-eyed Ford.

We all laughed. "That's a real song," he said. "I've heard it a lot at parties and get-togethers. There are lots more verses," he said. "They are all just like that. It starts with "I will take you home on my old gray mare" and it ends with "I will take you home in my one-eyed Ford."

"How about those words at the beginning?" I asked. It was awkward for me to refer to the Mesquakie language, generally referred to on the settlement as "speaking Indian."

James knew what I meant. "Those? Oh, they don't have any meaning. They're just a chant. Just something you say."

◇ 17 ◇

James North soon became a regular rider on my trips to the Mesquakie settlement. I had arranged my schedule so as to have both Friday and Monday — as well as the weekend — free for my field trips. But James did not seem to worry about his schedule. He was willing to skip the classes necessary to have a ride home Friday morning and a return ride to campus on Monday afternoon.

I soon discovered that James had very close ties on the settlement. He had given up a lucrative scholarship to return from California and attend the University of Iowa. "I really missed seeing fall come," he explained. The University of Iowa was eighty miles away but close enough so that he could keep in touch with his family regularly.

James's presence at Iowa was not conspicuous. He wore blue jeans and Western boots and his black hair — usually drawn back tightly — was no longer and no shorter than that of many other students. His room in the dormitory was filled with blues records and he often carried his guitar home for the weekend. "It must be difficult," I said to him one day, "having to live in two cultures that are so different."

But James merely shrugged. "It's not hard at all," he answered. "You just have to make both cultures *work* for you." He was silent a long time, looking out the window of the warm car at the ice-covered fields. Then he went on: "One time in school, we were studying about Darwin and the theory of evolution. I was home reading my book and I told my parents

about it. They really gave it to me. 'So you've become one of
the Monkey-men,' they said. 'You know that *our* people
weren't descended from monkeys.' "

It seemed like a contradiction to me. I knew that Mesquakies considered animals to be their relatives and their ancestors.
I didn't question him further, but I suspected that it was the
theory more than the evolution of species that disturbed them.

James looked out the window at the Iowa cornfields — now
with thick snow covering the scarecrow stubs. "You have to
know what is important to you," he said. "When I was in California, they had recorded messages. You know, you could dial
the telephone and get a prayer. That's not my idea of religion."

When he talked of other young native American poets, he
was often equally scornful. "He wrote a poem called 'Dog
Stew,' " he said in reference to one such poet. Without thinking, I laughed. It was an automatic response but James did not
see any humor. His eyes glared: "I could kill him," he said.

"Oh, I'm sorry," I said. "I didn't mean to laugh at something important to you. I didn't understand what you were
trying to say."

"That's okay," he said. "I know you didn't understand. But
he did. And that's what makes his poem inexcusable." The
poem was a fool-the-Anglos satire apparently written by an acculturated Indian who no longer took seriously the eating of
dog. For such people, James had little tolerance. He would
never be as overtly militant nor as covertly acculturated as such
Indians. Perhaps that was why he had no trouble moving between the two worlds in which he lived.

James was a talented poet who had published in good academic journals. When I first met him that afternoon in the
Iowa Memorial Union, I asked him about his poetry and he
responded by picking up a spiral notebook and showing me not

poems but drawings that he had sketched in pencil. They were in the abstract style characteristic of traditional native American art. In one corner was the jagged line that I immediately recognized as a symbol of lightning, but I feigned ignorance and asked James what it meant. "That? Oh, that's nothing. That's just something I felt like putting in."

James never talked much about his poems, but I had read them in the journals and I knew there were many references to his grandmother and the debt he owed to her. James did talk about his grandmother and in so doing he was perhaps getting at the very heart of his poetry.

As we drove down the snow-packed roads of the settlement, he pointed out to me the tiny shack in which she lived. It was the house where Harry Oster had stopped to ask directions that first day. "See those?" he said, pointing to the names Jimi Hendrix and B. B. King, scratched on outhouses that had puzzled Bob Sayre and me. "My brother and I did that. We're the only ones around here who listen to blues. People tell us, 'Why, that's black music!' But I still like it." He did not offer an explanation for the swastika and I did not ask.

Likewise, after that first time, I did not ask again to speak to James's grandmother, though I secretly yearned for him to offer an introduction. Her name was mentioned, although she was never quoted, in many of the old books I had read in the library. She was Maxine Buffalo Robe and she had important roles in many of the old ceremonies.

James spoke often of the many hours that he had spent, with his brother, at the home of his grandmother. And once he told me of his memory of his grandfather. His grandfather was also mentioned prominently in the old books and was an important member of the conservative Old Bear faction.

James seemed to wait until the proper moment to tell this story. We had just turned in to the settlement and were slowly making our way down the narrow, winding road. He looked straight ahead out of the front windshield and spoke in a voice that was softer than usual.

"You know, Freddy, they tell me I'm not supposed to remember this. I was too young at the time, but I do remember it. Maybe I dreamed it. I don't know but it's very clear in my mind.

"My grandfather was very sick, I know that. And we were at my grandparents' house. And I remember that my grandfather had to go to the toilet. And I remember my father and my uncle, James Youngman — you know James. The two of them carried my grandfather to the outhouse. I can remember seeing them carry him outside. The memory is very clear in my mind.

"And that night he died. And that's the last memory I have of my grandfather." The drone of the heater became conspicuously loud inside the car. "My mother says I was too young to remember," he said. Neither of us spoke again until I pulled up in front of his house.

More often, James told me lighthearted accounts of events that had happened to him and his brother as they were growing up. One incident remains very vivid in my mind, perhaps because it reminds me, in tone and style, of many of the Mesquakie trickster stories that I had read. Of course, James did not think of these anecdotes with the same kind of reverence and awe.

"You know one night, a bunch of us were out on a country road at night messing around. We had a couple of six-packs and were having a good time.

"When we saw the cop car coming, we scattered. We started running through the ditch and over fields. And the cop called to us to stop but we were scared.

"Then he started firing his gun at us and we were really scared. We hit the ground and we could hear those bullets whizzing over our heads.

"The others got away, but I had to crawl over those fields a long way before the cop gave up and quit shining his spotlight.

"Then I went home.

"But you know they had just put fertilizer on the fields — manure you know — and when I got up I had it all over my clothes. And I fell in a sewage ditch and I got even more shit all over me.

"So I had to walk home that way. And it got real cold and by the time I got home, it had frozen. So when I got home, I had frozen shit all over me. And I had to peel it off with a screwdriver." His story had taken us through a complete range of emotions and we were both laughing loudly as we drove rapidly between frozen cornfields.

"I wrote a poem about that story," James said.

"Really?" I was teaching a course called "The Idea of Comedy" and I thought the poem would be an excellent contribution. "Do you think I could see a copy of the poem? Or could you read it for my class?"

"No," James answered. "I don't have any extra copies."

James's poems are all translations. "I hear the poem in Indian," he explained, "then I have to translate it into English. It is very difficult because there are some words that *you* just don't have and there are others that just can't be translated. You know in the Raccoon and the Wolf story, when the Raccoon is in the tree pushing off bark and he says he is just stretching his legs? Well, that is *one word* in our language. It's a very beautiful word and it has many meanings. But I could never explain it in English."

"What is the word in Mesquakie?" I asked.

James shook his head.

I asked James North if he could teach me Mesquakie. "I would pay you five dollars an hour," I said.

"How about ten?" he said with a laugh.

Then, more seriously: "Why do you want to know the language? It's very hard to learn." Silence. Then, "Maybe I could try to teach you the language."

Several times I have heard James North sing. At Mesquakie Powwows, he is nearly always among the select group — mostly older men — who sit in the center around the drum and blend their voices in high- and low-pitched chants while others dance around the circle — the women in short, mincing steps, the men with flourishing knee and elbow action. I could never separate James's voice from that of the other men and, of course, I could not understand the words. But when I listened closely and let myself relax I could hear many voices — the voices of the birds and beasts of the universe, singing in unison.

It was a language that was not easily taught. Mesquakies say that it was *given* to them.

◇ 18 ◇

James North was for me a sort of mirror; through him I could see how I was perceived on the settlement. "By now, everybody has probably noticed that one-eyed Ford that keeps driving up and down our roads," he said the first time he rode to the settlement with me. "I'm sure they all have theories about who you are and what you are doing. My brother asked me last week who you were, and I told him you were doing research on stories. I told him you were all right."

Then on a later trip: "I'll bet by now everyone has a name for you, Freddy."

"What is it?"

"Don't you know?" he laughed. Then, rubbing his chin, "I'll bet they call you Furry Face. What do you think?"

I was embarrassed to see myself reflected through someone else's eyes. But I wanted to learn from James North how I should behave in my relationships with people on the settlement. "Is there anything I might do that would turn people off — things I might not even notice?" I asked.

James laughed. "Yeah, I remember when I brought my roommate from California home with me last Christmas. My mom and dad said there were lots of things he did that really turned them off. Just little things. But right now I can't remember what they were." That was as much as he would tell me.

I sensed that James was, in his own way, "doing research on stories." We were fellow travelers on the same road, but he knew the road so much better that he could quietly laugh at me as I bumped around from tree to tree, knocking on doors and asking for stories.

For hours, he would sit, silent, on the long ride between Tama and Iowa City. Then, suddenly, he would volunteer, without my asking, an important piece of information about a story or a tradition. One day, he volunteered this observation about the whole body of Mesquakie stories that were recorded in William Jones's book. "You know," he said, "if there is one thing that happens again and again in those stories, it's that somebody or something is being eaten." I thought of the raccoons or the mouse eating the heart of the deer. And for some reason I thought of the huge chunks of meat on the platter in the Sturgeons' house. "It's like what they say you should do when you get a splinter in your finger. When you get it out, you're supposed to eat it."

"Why is that?"

"I don't know. I guess so it won't come back to haunt you again."

James was often helpful, but I was still shocked when one day he volunteered the name of a potential informant. "You want to know stories, don't you?" he asked. Then, before I could answer: "Have you talked with Tom Youngman?"

"You mean James?"

"No, Tom. Have you talked to him?"

"No, I haven't. Should I?"

"I think he knows many stories," James said. For the rest of the trip he was silent, almost secretive. I could not tell what he was thinking. As he got out of the car, I quickly got directions to Tom Youngman's house.

There were at least three or four inches of fresh snow on the ground. The mailbox at the road told me that I had found the lane to Tom Youngman's house, but as soon as I turned into it, I could see that the lane dropped sharply downhill, curving through a thick timber. Quickly, I stopped the car, knowing I could never make it back up that steep incline. In fact, it might be too late already, I thought, as I pulled the emergency brake tight.

Even by foot, the way to Tom Youngman's house was treacherous. I half slid and half ran down the hill, the bitterly cold wind whipping at my coat. The house at the bottom was a tiny one, and I expected to find within a very old man — perhaps as old as Maxine Buffalo Robe. My hand ached with cold when I took off my glove for only a minute to knock at the roughly hewn door. It was several minutes before it opened. A thin man, perhaps thirty-five years old, with a tiny pointed goatee stepped out and closed the door behind him. I might have barged right into the house, just as the Turtle had barged into the lodge, had the man not acted so quickly to bar my way.

"I'm looking for Tom Youngman," I shouted above the wind.

"I'm Tom Youngman," he said softly.

"Oh." It was too cold for me to take the time to explain my project carefully, but I quickly introduced myself. "I was told that you might be able to help me out with some information about stories."

The man's deep brown eyes looked into mine for several minutes. I sensed in his eyes a power and a calmness that I was not at all familiar with. He was wearing only a flannel shirt, but he did not even shiver in the cold, piercing wind. As he stood in front of the closed door, looking deeply into my eyes, he somehow put me at ease, and I felt neither the fear nor the guilt that I usually felt when first meeting people on the Mesquakie settlement. His silence was an adequate communication and when he finally spoke, I knew what he was about to say.

"I can't tell you stories," he said softly. I had no trouble hearing him over the whistling wind. "I use my stories to pray. To me, they are sacred."

I thanked him, and he opened the door again and retreated

into his small lodge. The smell and warmth of a wood fire rushed out at me in the split second that the door was open and then I was left shivering in the piercing wind.

With great difficulty, I managed to climb back up the steep incline and back my Ford out of the slippery lane.

The next week when I called James North to see if he needed a ride home, he asked about my visit: "Hey, did you go see that man I told you about?"

"Who was that?"

"That man I told you about — Tom Youngman."

"Oh, yes. I did."

"Did you talk to him? Did he tell you any stories?"

"No, he didn't want to tell me any stories. He said they were sacred to him."

"Oh." He laughed. "I thought he might tell you some stories." By his laugh, I knew what I had already suspected. James North had tricked me.

For a couple of hours, I was hurt and angry. Then I thought about the story of the Raccoon and the Wolf and I had my own theory about Mesquakie stories: it seems that in nearly every story, somebody or some thing is tricked and by being tricked learns a lesson.

19

JAMES NORTH was intrigued by William Jones's book, *Fox Texts*, and he examined it carefully each time we traveled between Iowa City and Tama. It was as if there was something particularly fascinating about seeing stories he considered oral written down on the printed page. I felt much the same way when I discovered that a person I had read about, such as Maxine Buffalo Robe, truly existed in a little house that I drove past several times a week. For me, there was something exotic in seeing what was written come to life.

"You know that story about the Turtle," James said one day. "My parents recited it for me almost word for word as it is here."

I nodded but tried not to act overanxious.

"My mother said the Turtle was created before Man, but he was thrown back into the mud because he was too ugly. She said that if others had been like him, the world would not be as good a place to live."

The remark confused me even more. Why should Henry Sturgeon use a creature so ugly to attempt to teach me a lesson? What did the Turtle know that I did not?

I found no satisfactory answers, but James's remark convinced me even more that the oral traditions of the Mesquakies were still very much alive. Mesquakies still tell and live a history that extends back to the creation of the Turtle and beyond, down to the mudholes of the water. I now knew there was nothing at all strange about seeing B. B. King's name inscribed on an outhouse that had been used by a respected

Mesquakie elder. I could see Maxine Buffalo Robe sitting in her tiny lodge making fry bread in front of a colored TV screen. It was an image of continuity through change.

Back in 1916, Truman Michelson had warned that with the "passing of the older generation" the stories and traditions would be forever lost; fifty-five years later, they were still very much alive. At the same time, James's interest in the book and his inclination to write and publish poetry was an indication that the younger generation was more closely tied to the written word. I wanted to find a way of keeping the oral traditions alive for those who had been trained to respect the power of the written word.

I envisioned a textbook to be used in the day school, and James North seemed to be the ideal person to translate and re-translate stories for it. With the help of his family and friends, he could choose the stories that should be included and provide whatever commentary he felt was needed to teach Mesquakie children about the complexities of their language and culture. James's sensitivity to language and his ties to the most traditional elements of his culture made him the ideal person for the task. I could provide technical assistance and perhaps write an introduction that might satisfy some of the requirements for my Ph.D.

Before talking to James, I wanted to discuss my ideas with Lucille Waters. It was too cold to sit in the yard, now white snow sprinkled with puppy tracks. I sat with Lucille and her husband, John, in a tiny living room around a fuel-oil space heater.

She nodded as I talked; she agreed that James would be ideal for the job. "His grandmother, you know, has a lot of knowledge — as much as anyone on the settlement."

John Waters sat silently. I sensed his disapproval but was not sure.

I asked Lucille if her youth culture group would be able to

help collect stories from their parents and grandparents. "No," she answered. "The stories *belong* to the older people. They know how to tell them and it is up to them to decide whether they want to give them away." Her husband nodded his agreement.

I was puzzled. What did this mean about James North and his participation? Lucille Waters shrugged. "You'll just have to discover that for yourself. It is up to him and his grandmother. You can ask him. That might be your best bet."

Lucille Waters was smiling. Her husband sat beside her, silent.

James North borrowed my copy of *Fox Texts,* which I had obtained through interlibrary loan from the University of Indiana. He borrowed it for a night, then a weekend, then for the Christmas vacation. I had to return the book to the University of Indiana, but first I had it photocopied and loaned him the copy indefinitely. Finally, I summoned the courage to tell him my plan and ask him to help.

As I talked, I found it very hard to explain why the project was important. I felt paternalistic and the more I talked, the less convinced I was in my own mind that the oral stories should be put on the printed page. James was silent as I talked and I felt extremely uncomfortable with his silence. Finally, I gave up and we rode in silence the rest of the trip. As I dropped him at the front door of his house, James gave me the answer I had waited for earlier. "That might work out, Freddy. I just don't know. Let me think about it for a while. I'll let you know. Okay?"

And he was gone, his dog leaping at his legs as he ran through the snow, his suitcase bouncing along at his side.

It was three months later that I got the answer from James and in the meantime I pretended to be patient.

One morning in his dormitory room, rubbing his eyes in an

attempt to wake up, he gave me his reply. "You know that thing you talked to me about? I just can't do it. I've given it a lot of thought but I just can't do it." He picked up the photocopied book and handed it to me. "You know I've read those stories and they're just not the same. I remember hearing the Raccoon and the Wolf story when I was little. It was much funnier and much more real. That just doesn't come across when you read it in a book."

He thought a minute. "I'm not saying it shouldn't be done. But *I* can't do it."

The next silence was much longer and he looked at the floor. Then he looked up and smiled. "I'm glad I decided not to do it."

It was precisely the response that I expected. As he talked to me I could, in my imagination, see two images of James North. One had white clay on the face and it was smiling at me. The other was painted black with charcoal and it was expressionless and silent. Then the two images merged and I saw one face — painted with bands of black and white.

20

I CONTINUED to talk with Henry Sturgeon, but the visits became less productive and I was still impatient to find that definitive source of information. "Have you talked with Charlie Laveur?" Mr. Sturgeon asked one day. "My uncle told me everything I know, but he died early and I always feel as if something is missing, that my knowledge is incomplete. I think Charlie Laveur could teach you more than I could."

So on a cold, damp morning in mid-January, I began my search for the house of Charlie Laveur. As was common in Iowa, we had experienced a January thaw and the snow cover had washed away into black mud that clings to your boots. The warm weather had been a welcome interruption of the subzero temperatures, but now it was getting cold again. The snow was gone and the dampness still on the ground, but a wind was whipping across Iowa. It felt much chillier than the temperature indicated.

The directions I had been given were simple and I followed them carefully — steering my car down the main road past the Clouds's house, then taking the first road to the right. It was a road I had never traveled before and I drove about a mile before I came to the first clearing. The mailbox indicated that it was not the house I was looking for, and I continued to drive — weaving to the left and to the right, up and down hills. By now, I was totally disoriented. I drove past several houses and checked the names on the mailboxes, but none belonged to Charles Laveur. Finally, the road forked and I found myself back on the familiar main road. Apparently I had, without knowing it, traveled in a huge semicircle.

Again I began my search, this time looking more carefully for the road I was supposed to take. But the first road to the right was indeed the one I had taken before, and once again I made my semicircular journey, checking every mailbox very carefully but failing to find the house I was looking for. Again, I was back on the main road, near where I had begun.

Finally, in desperation, I parked my car beside the road and began my search on foot. Although there were definitely no other roads to the right, there was a very narrow lane leading through the woods down a steep hill. No mailbox was in sight, but I decided to try the lane anyway.

As I rounded a curve, I could see down at the bottom, almost half a mile away, a small white frame house with smoke trailing from the chimney. The house was on flat land, with no trees, but some distance behind it was a thick line of trees — perhaps indicating the banks of the Iowa River. This might be the "road" to Charlie Laveur's house, but I could see that I had been wise to leave my car behind. There were deep ruts in this narrow lane that would soon be frozen into the texture of the earth. Stepping carefully along the ruts, I made my way down the lane toward the solitary house in the distance.

The ground had already begun to harden in places and the ruts jerked at my ankles. Elsewhere, it was still soggy and I could feel my boot heels sinking into the claylike earth. Soon the land opened to my left on to a relatively flat and clear area that looked as if corn or some other crop had been recently harvested. The land sloped gently down to the house. To my right was a heavy timber, much like the woods beside Lucille Waters' house where I had walked with my wife and sons months earlier. However, I could see no trace of a path through these woods.

The wind was whipping my topcoat around my legs. I

turned up my coat collar, lowered my head, and walked quickly — my body tense and shivering. The cold wind at my back forced my attention rigidly on the goal at the bottom of the hill. I was anxious to get inside that warm house.

About halfway down the lane, I stopped. I thought I had heard something, a vague roaring sound somewhat like the blowing of the wind yet more definite and articulate. It was a very definite sound like nothing I had heard before. I examined the ground on all sides of me and I looked up at the tops of the trees. Something had made me stop, almost against my will. But I could not be sure; maybe it was the wind or maybe I had imagined it.

I was still shivering but I continued to stand there in the wind, listening carefully and looking out across the clearing to my left. The timber was directly behind me and I could feel its presence vividly.

By now, the sound that had stopped me was not important. In the land to my left and the woods behind me was a feeling that demanded attention. As anxious as I was to get inside that warm house, I felt compelled to listen and to look. There were spirits in the land, I had been told, the spirits of the people, animals, plants, dreams, and stories that belonged to this piece of ground. I was romantic enough to accept and believe the mysticism of the Mesquakies. But it was still mysticism. Until now.

I guess I had read too many of the religious texts collected by Truman Michelson. They were all bound in the drab green with gold lettering of the Bureau of American Ethnology. Nearly all of the texts were stories concerning origins. A young man had a certain experience that moved him and puzzled him and he fasted for a number of days so that an answer could be given to him. And when he had fasted, he was visited by a spirit who told him of the origin of his experience and who advised him as to what he should do in the present and future. This kind of personal experience had been transformed into cultural rituals that were still performed. Like the stories told to me by Henry and Isabel Sturgeon, these origin myths moved fluidly between present, past, and future. As I stood there on the lane, I could see the printing on the page and I could hear the archaic language.

The wind had stopped for a minute and I could smell the dampness in the air. My feet were soggy with melted snow, but I knew that underneath the earth was frozen solid. As I stood there listening and waiting, I could sense the incredible age of the land on which I was standing. Imbedded in the land were experiences from the past and spirits to guide a person through the present and future. I had never been here before and I did not really know where I was, but I knew that this was a very special place with very special feelings. This was the place that Mrs. Sturgeon meant when she talked about the very center of the island.

I stood there for several minutes. Then I resumed my walk down the hill and knocked on the door of the white frame house. After several minutes, an elderly woman came to the door. Looking out the glass pane, she noticeably started when she saw my pale, bearded face. She shook her head vigorously and spoke to me, but I could not hear. Then she opened the door, just a crack.

"I am looking for Charles Laveur." I shouted to make myself heard above the wind.

She said nothing, just pointed past my shoulder to the right. Across the lane, in a large clearing in the woods, was another white frame house with a large rectangular wickiup beside it.

"Is that Charles Laveur's house?" I shouted.

She nodded, then closed the door.

I later learned who the woman was: Charles Laveur's sister, one of the few people on the settlement designated to grow the sacred Indian tobacco.

21

Except for the wickiup beside it, Charlie Laveur's house looked very much like the typical Iowa farmhouse. A circular drive, deeply rutted, led from the lane up to the porch, which extended almost the entire length of the house. An old station wagon was parked to one side of this drive, on the grass. As usual, the dogs were ever-present. They greeted me with tentative wags of their tails and sniffed at my heels as I walked up onto the rickety wooden porch.

As I knocked, I could hear the commotion of small children playing inside. And then from deep within, a loud, high-pitched shout: "Come in!" Still cautious from my encounter with the timid woman across the lane, I knocked again — hoping the voice might realize that I was a stranger. But again from deep within came the shout: "Come in!" I opened the door slowly and stood for a minute in the doorway, surveying the chaotic scene that is inevitable when four preschool children are playing seriously on the floor. For a minute, I saw only the children. The smell of dirty diapers was strong. Then from the right side of the room, the same high-pitched voice: "Come in."

Charlie Laveur was a short, somewhat round man with a white bristly beard and twinkling eyes. Dressed in jeans and a T-shirt, he was sitting on a couch beside a very warm fuel-oil space heater. Most of his teeth were missing and he was grinning at me with an open mouth and a directness that I had come not to expect on the Mesquakie settlement. I stood before him, ill at ease, in the middle of the floor and told him that Henry Sturgeon had mentioned his name.

"Oh, yes. John Sturgeon. You know him at the University."

"No, it's Henry Sturgeon . . . I've been . . ."

But it was no use. It was apparently unimportant to Charles Laveur who had sent me and what exactly I wanted. He had something he wanted to tell me. Speaking quickly and without pause, he told me again the story of the Man with a Beard and he rubbed his own white whiskers and pointed at my own. "They keep your face warm, don't they!" He laughed. I had never before seen an Indian with a full beard.

I now knew the story was an old one. Among the Inca, Chibchan, Mayan, and Nahuatl peoples, there are stories of a human god who lived among the people and established the present order, then departed. This person was clothed in white cloth or paint, came from the East, and wore a beard. When the Europeans arrived, the name for this god was applied to them and later became a part of native terminology. From Chile to the Rio Grande, the story of a man with fair skin and a beard is common. I have heard the same story from a member of another Indian tribe in Montana and the Mesquakie version was printed once in an official program for the Powwow.

The story was authentic, but as Charlie Laveur told it to me, rubbing his own beard and smiling, I felt even more sure that the story referred directly to me. I was at the same time both the first and the last man with a beard to visit them, and he seemed to be telling me what that first and last man should know.

"Across the water, your people had a vision that they would find a friend. They saw a man with one arm, who lived in the center of the island. With help he could rule the whole island." I could sense his eyes probing for a reaction from me as he talked of broken promises: "The cannon was fired eight times to God when the promises were made but the white man has forgotten. There is the same God — he doesn't forget. We are still friends but the white man forgets his promises." He waved his arm in a broad arc — presumably toward the East. But I was still disoriented. He continued, "The treaties are all in Washington. The white man has them. He knows the Indian will remember. If you don't remember, you're not a Mesquakie."

Mr. Laveur's rolling speech and fluid gestures had an eloquence that commanded respect. With his toothless smile and his white-bearded stubble, he made a particularly striking figure. I no longer noticed any of the chaos that had struck me when I entered.

I did notice, however, that the room was extremely hot. Sweat was rolling down my forehead, but I did not feel I should take off my heavy topcoat — at least right now. I remembered what Mr. Sturgeon had told me about the discipline of listening to stories. I was trying hard to use my brain as he had suggested, to imprint the story on my memory as it might be recorded on a tape recorder. But as I tried, it was difficult to listen carefully to what Mr. Laveur was saying.

"When the white man first came here, he was hungry, so the Indian said, 'Go out and hunt animals — get deer, pheasant, and turkey. Go get corn and squash.' And he said, 'Go get food and feed the white man.' And it was done.

"But now *you* say the white man fed the Indian. Not true." He chuckled as he reminded himself of the contradiction. I thought of my student who had told me about the Indians and their welfare checks.

Mr. Laveur was talking very slowly, but he did not pause and I knew that I should listen and not interrupt. He seemed to move abruptly from one subject to another, but his progression was not chronological. In fact, he seemed to move deeper and deeper into the past. "Where was man created? Right here.

We know lots of things." His toothless smile was again laughing at my ignorance. "When it first started, there were two — a red one and a green one. Human beings. The red one, that was the Fox and the green one, that was the Bear." My mind jumped. Were they human beings or animals? I suspected he was talking about the Fox clan, from one part of which the War Chief is chosen, and the Bear clan, from which the hereditary Chief — who is always peaceful — is chosen. I remembered reading in one of the books that red is the special paint of the Fox clan, green, the special paint of the Bear clan.

Mr. Laveur's hands were moving together as if he were molding with clay. "The spirit created the first one — that was the green one. And another spirit created another one. He thought he would be lonely so he took the flesh from his side — yes from his arm — and he created the other one."

Now Charlie Laveur jumped quickly to another story. This one I had heard from John Sturgeon and I had read it in William Jones's book. "You know when the French first met our people they were coming along the river bank and they said, 'Who are you?'

"And we said, 'We are Foxes.' And it was true for those people were members of the Fox clan.

"And ever since, we have been known as Fox Indians, but we are not. We are Mesquakies. Because we were created from the Red Earth and we were the very first people created."

I thought about my experience a few minutes earlier on the lane and I wondered if that was the key to remembering as Henry Sturgeon had told me I must remember. If you feel the spirits that are in the land, then you can feel the creation and you can remember without trying.

I was thinking about the land and the way my father had longed to return to the farm. It was as if Mr. Laveur could read my mind. He was smiling.

"We told the white man to leave all but six inches. And what does he do today? He plows the ground and he doesn't leave all but six inches. And when he buries a man, what does he do? He doesn't leave all but the six inches.

"The top six inches is for man. That you can plow. The rest belongs to God." His hands were moving gently, one caressing the other.

"When we eat food, we must give thanks first to the spirits — give a sacrifice to God.

"Also when people die, we must talk to the spirits. We must throw tobacco in the grave and pray to the earth to remember what was promised to God. We put little trees on the top and we throw tobacco.

"We tell the trees to remember what was promised to God."

When he used the word "promise" he gave it a heavy stress and seemed to probe more deeply into my eyes. When he and Henry Sturgeon had told me that the white man had forgotten his promises, I assumed they were referring to the specific promises made in all of those infamous treaties. I knew those promises had not been kept. Now Mr. Laveur was talking about another kind of promise — a promise made much earlier, a promise of harmony between all living and nonliving things on the earth. He was talking about the white man who had separated himself from the earth and hence could not remember his creation.

My father loved the land very much, and so do the Amish and Mennonite farmers who lived near me in Iowa. Their plows penetrated deeply into the soil and their combines gobbled the corn from the fields. They sought harmony with the land but they had never talked of these promises. They did not consider the earth to be their grandmother.

Now Mr. Laveur was talking about my religion in much the same terms Mr. Sturgeon had used: "The white man tells about God and Christ, but today there are all different sects and they are all opposed." He was not referring just to the Protestant sects but to a more abstract lack of unity in the religion of my people. Then he seemed to contradict himself in the next breath. "The white man has only God and Christ, but we have many spirits. The earth is a spirit — she is our grandmother. The snow is a spirit, the trees are spirits. The moon is a spirit too — it is the wolf. And the sun is our grandfather." Could it be possible that the Mesquakies' religion, with its many spirits, is more unified, more monotheistic than my Judeo-Christian culture? There were many spirits, but they were all relatives. Perhaps that is the secret that the earth holds for those who remember clearly.

Charlie Laveur had been talking for more than half an hour and I had not said a word. My mind was working furiously and I had momentarily forgotten my discomfort. My coat was of heavy wool and sweat was pouring down my face while outside the wind was whistling around the house. Mr. Laveur did not seem to notice.

When his wife and daughter returned from the grocery store, carrying heavy paper sacks into the kitchen, they shouted at Mr. Laveur in Mesquakie and he shouted back, almost without interrupting his conversation to me. When he finished speaking I had a chance to remove my coat and find a more comfortable position on my straight chair. I had just gotten comfortable when there was a loud knock on the door. Charlie Laveur picked up a wool C.P.O. shirt and was putting it on as he walked to the door. The knocking continued, but he didn't answer.

As the door opened, a cold burst of wind exploded into the room and I reached for my coat. It was the game warden, standing stiff and formal in his official state uniform. "I've got a deer," he said, pointing to his station wagon in the drive. "It was hit by a car out on the highway last night and it's been there overnight." He looked at Charlie Laveur, who was already preparing to go out in the cold. "You should be able to get the skin and give the meat to the dogs."

I pulled on my coat and followed the warden and Charlie Laveur outside. The dogs were standing around the opened back door of the station wagon, eyeing the stiff legs pointing out in the air. Together, the three of us lifted the stiff deer out of the station wagon and carried her to the far entrance of the wickiup beside the house. The body was very stiff, yet at the same time almost soft under my gloves. We placed it on a large wooden platform, then stood back and surveyed the impressive form.

22

Aꜰᴛᴇʀ ᴛʜᴇ game warden left, Charlie Laveur and I stood silently looking at the body of the deer on the table. It was a large doe, her head thrown back gracefully, even as she lay frozen in death. I could see her standing in the middle of the highway, sniffing into the breeze, quivering, wary of danger yet unable to escape from the overpowering automobile with its glaring headlights.

Charlie Laveur reached out and stroked the deer's body affectionately, and, almost as if he were talking to himself, explained about the powers of the deer. "The deer has four eyes," he said pointing to a spot on the back of the head. It was not rational, but I could understand the deer's power to see both in front and behind. She could see the past and remember the future. "And she also has four ears," he explained. "Two are back here." And he pointed to the delicate yet strong tendon that ran along the edge of the hind leg. I ran my fingers lightly along the tendon, as he showed me; I could almost feel her trembling power. "When someone comes up from behind, the deer can hear it right here and the deer can see too."

The wolf is a hunter who bounds powerfully after his prey in the broad daylight, howling and barking in delight at the chase. The deer is a creature of prey, sometimes open and generous in taking passengers across the river. But as the turtle discovered, she is not an easy prey and she is not passive.

The deer lying dead before us brought to mind a story that I

had read in William Jones's book. It was about a Deer, lying
dead in the forest. Four animals — an Eagle, a Panther, a Tarantula, and an anonymous fourth — were gathered around
the body, arguing loudly.

They were quarreling over the division of the Deer. One
wanted this part, another wanted that, and they had not yet
come to an agreement when the man appeared in their midst.
Then they suddenly fell into silence. Presently the man put
questions to them. "Tarantula, did you kill it?" "No." "Eagle,
did you kill it?" "No." "Panther, did you kill it?" "No." "And
did you kill it?" "No."
He found on further questioning that they had found the
Deer already dead, but he did not learn who had found it first.
Then he upbraided them for their quarreling. At the same
time, he began to cut up the Deer in four equal shares.
The way he did was to split the Deer in half from the head to
the tail, then each half was cut in two again. He gave a part to
each of the four, and they went their several ways feeling kindly
toward one another and to the man who had settled their dispute.

As I looked at the deer on the table, I could see the line drawn
through the body — from north to south and from east to west.
There was something about the body that seemed to cast a spell
on me. I did not move or talk.

Mr. Laveur interrupted my reverie. "There is a funny thing
about the deer," he said. "If you shoot an arrow into a deer,
the deer can sometimes shoot the arrow right back to you. If
the arrow hits in the right place." He pointed to a particular
spot on the left rear flank of the creature. I must have looked
dubious, for he quickly added. "It's true! I have seen it happen."

I was not a hunter and I was appalled by the men in brown
jackets who trampled through the cornfields near our farmhouse every fall — flushing out pheasants and shooting them.

Charlie Laveur did not look like a hunter to me, just as James Youngman did not look like an artist. He knew the deer and respected its powers and perhaps that was what made him a good hunter. Maybe it was I, not the men in brown jackets, who was ignorant about the nature of the hunt.

We were in a large rectangular lodge built of planks and covered with a lightweight tarpaulin. The floor was earth and there were two small open fires, one near each end of the long structure. Both fires were burning slowly and smoke rolled from each up through smoke holes in the roof. I had read in Michelson's books about the Mesquakie spirit known as "He-Who-Lies-with-Eyes-Bulging-Through-the-Smoke-Hole." It was a strange word, so long and hyphenated, and Michelson admitted that the translation was difficult, if not impossible. The name had an archaic ring that had amused me in the library. Now, as I watched the smoke hole, I could see the word flashing before my eyes, long and hyphenated, almost like a visual chant.

It was some time before I realized that Charlie Laveur was talking to me. He was looking at the fire nearest us and explaining: "That's an Indian fire. It was started in the old way, with flint, and you are never to throw a match in the fire. It never goes out, you keep it going. But when someone dies, you let it go out, wait four days, and then start another fire."

Fire was also a spirit, the books told me. I knew that Indian tobacco is thrown into the fire and prayers are made to the spirit of the fire and the spirit of the smoke hole, powerful spirits who can spread the message to other spirits. This fire was much smaller than the one I had imagined when I read the book. I worried that it might go out; surely, the burden of keeping the fire was a heavy one. I had an urge to add another log, to coax the fire into blazing life. But Charlie Laveur was not at all worried. Very deliberately, he picked up one log and moved it almost imperceptibly. Around the fire was a thick blanket of charcoal, fire that had recently lived. It was this charcoal, I presumed, that was used to blacken the face when one went into the woods to fast.

Stories were told around fires and William Jones said that the storyteller often blackened his face with charcoal. As I stood around the fire, I felt as if I were experiencing a story — being told in a language that is beyond words. A visual chant without sound that curled its way up through the smoke hole above me. The wind was whipping the tarpaulin against the lodge just as it had whipped my topcoat against my legs an hour earlier in the lane. The wind was getting colder every minute and one end of the lodge was open, but I did not feel cold. The slow-burning fire was radiating an incredible warmth.

I noticed that Charlie Laveur was wearing only a C.P.O. shirt over his T-shirt. "This is *my* place," he said proudly, and swept his arm in a wide arc to include the pelts and skinned bodies of small animals hanging from lines above and around us.

Directly in front of me was a skunk, unskinned but half-frozen. He pointed to it and explained, "Let it thaw. Cook it and eat it and you'll never catch the sniffles all winter."

"What are those?" I asked, pointing to a row of small animals, already skinned, hanging from a line. They seemed to be the animals that Bob Sayre and I had noticed that first day in the clearing around the house of Maxine Buffalo Robe.

"Those are muskrat."

"Do you eat them?"

"Oh yes. Rats are better than chicken. Very good. And then there are a couple of squirrels. But it is bad to kill them unless you really need them."

When I had walked through the woods, I had seen no animals. Here in Charlie Laveur's lodge, I was surrounded by animals of all kinds — reflections of the world outside.

I wanted to talk, to ask questions, but Mr. Laveur did not have the time or the inclination to tell me about all of the animals and objects in his lodge. He moved quickly through the long building, and I followed him to the far end, where a roughly cut plywood door opened into yet another part of the structure. As we walked through the door, warm air rushed out at us.

"This is where I live," he said proudly, closing the door behind us. It was a smaller version of the wickiup, made of the same planks and canvas with a small, wood-burning stove in the very center of the floor. This inner lodge seemed to be square rather than oblong. Along each side were the same raised platforms and, on one of these platforms, I presumed, Charlie Laveur slept. Again, there was a hole in the ceiling for smoke to escape, but the room was smaller and tighter; the stove kept it very warm, even the earth floor. "That house is where my daughter lives," he said, pointing to the white frame house that provided one wall of this section of the lodge. "But I live *here*."

He picked up a small container, opened it, and showed me what appeared to be loose tea. "Here is our tobacco," he said. "It is sacred. My sister who lives next door — maybe you saw her — she grows it. She has grown it since she was old enough not to have babies. Only one or two people grow it. Others must sacrifice something to get it. It started with this tribe when we were created. We use it in ceremonies; we throw it in the fire, and then we can talk to the spirits." He handled the container with respect, and I felt an awe for the power of what he was showing me. So it was the timid woman next door who grew tobacco. Somehow I felt that Charlie Laveur knew that I had visited her house in my search for him.

But he had no time for questions. He was still talking rapidly. "When a woman has the sickness, she knows she cannot come in my place," he said. I made a mental note not to bring Donna with me on such occasions.

"How about your wife then?" I asked. "Does she have to stay away too?"

Charlie Laveur laughed loudly. "My wife? She is seventy-two years old! She doesn't have the sickness anymore!" He grabbed my arm and laughed again, as if I were playing a joke on him. I felt extremely stupid.

He put the container away and pointed high up on the wall above the door. "I am a member of the Eagle clan. That is my sacred bundle." It was high on the wall and I looked up at it for several minutes, sensing its age and power. Of course, I could see only the outside cover, but I knew that the objects inside were probably older than anything I had seen in my life. They were objects that had been touched by people who had lived hundreds, perhaps thousands, of years before.

Now I knew why Lucille Waters had laughed when she told me about "The White Owl Sacred Pack" that had been foisted upon Michelson. It did not really matter whether the bundle was authentic. Anyone could see that this room was where the Eagle clan bundle belonged. This was where it had lived for many, many years, and it was out of place in Washington, D.C. Taken out of this lodge, placed in a museum behind a glass case, it would have no power. It would be totally useless, a joke.

I had been lost, and I had traveled down a long lane to Charlie Laveur's house. Now I was at the very heart of a lodge and I was being shown a sacred bundle that had its origin long ago and that had lived through many subsequent creations. It had been to Kansas and it had come back to Iowa. The fire had gone out and had been rekindled many times during the lifetime of this bundle. I felt very small in its presence.

I do not know why Charlie Laveur had shown me these sacred objects. Even at a distance they held a power that I had never before experienced. There was no rational explanation for Mr. Laveur's openness and my experience told me that his action ran counter to the nature of most Mesquakies. Perhaps Charlie Laveur was a particularly open person; perhaps he was merely in an especially good mood. Yet I knew that he would never be careless about his religion, and I felt that somehow my experience outside his house might have prepared me to make this journey without disturbing the friendly spirits who dwelled in and around the lodge — spirits with whom Mesquakies have maintained sacred bonds and promises from the beginning. I was by no means qualified to be a Mesquakie or share their beliefs, but for a few hours that afternoon I felt that I had passed into a friendly relation with the manitous.

As I was standing on the earth floor, near the stove, a small mouse crawled slowly out from under one of the platforms and walked around my feet. I had never seen a mouse walk so nonchalantly, and I was totally taken aback when it stood up on its hind legs and looked at me, almost as if it were trying to stare me in the eyes. I looked at the mouse for a long time, entranced, until it finally turned around and walked away.

Mr. Laveur was watching me and laughing. "I think he is sick," he said, apparently referring to the mouse. "Maybe I should hit him on the head with a stick." He laughed but made no move to get a stick. He then grabbed a brown sweater from one of the platforms, pulled it on over his bristly white hair, and opened the plywood door, letting in a gust of cold air.

"I have to go now," he said. "I have to get to work. I have to go down to the river."

"Can I talk to you again?" I asked.

"Oh, maybe so," he said.

"Can I come back next Friday?"

"Okay."

"What time would be good for you?"

"Oh, maybe one o'clock."

And immediately he was off, heading with purpose down to the river. He waved as he strolled off into the woods, leaving me standing in front of the carcass of the deer.

23

CHARLIE LAVEUR was truly the most exotic Mesquakie I had met. Friends were amazed when I told them that a Mesquakie lived in a wickiup through Iowa's subzero winters. I could never reproduce the feelings of awe I had experienced in his lodge, feelings I wanted to share with Donna.

When I returned the next Friday at one o'clock to keep my appointment with Charlie Laveur, he was not at home. His daughter in the white frame house told me he had just left for the river bank. Again and again, I returned to see him, alone and with Donna, but could not find him at home.

One day, many weeks later, I heard loud talking behind the door of his inner lodge. When I knocked, I was greeted with a loud "Come in." I opened the door to find Charlie Laveur and four younger Mesquakie men standing around the stove in the middle of the floor. They were all dressed in mackinaw jackets and they were talking and laughing together in Mesquakie. They continued their conversation for a minute even after I had opened the door. Then they paused suddenly, and I was left the center of attention — embarrassed and ill at ease. They were all looking at me, and I looked at Charlie Laveur. He smiled but did not speak. It was at least fifteen degrees below zero that day and the ground even inside the wickiup was like granite. Behind me, I could feel the frigid wind; in front, the warm air radiated by the wood-burning stove. The smell of burning wood was strong.

I did not know what to say. I thought I should leave, but I

did not know how I could do so gracefully. Finally, I blurted out a comment about the weather. Mr. Laveur chuckled toothlessly and rubbed his white, bristly beard. "Ah, but I know. You will keep your face warm." Then all of the men laughed, and I tried to laugh with them. It was a feeble attempt and I felt even more like the outsider.

Mr. Laveur looked more serious and swung his arm in a wide arc, indicating the men around the stove. "I am busy," he said, dividing the second word into two syllables and giving it heavy stress. "Maybe you could come back next week at one o'clock." I knew that I would have trouble finding him again, but I welcomed the chance to leave without seeming rude.

As I turned to leave, a mouse wandered out from under one of the platforms and again walked around my feet. It was maybe the same mouse that had danced for me several weeks before. While I paused, it walked slowly around me and then back to its place under the platform. All of the men were quiet as they watched me. When I looked up at them, they all laughed loudly and I laughed with them. Mr. Laveur swung his arm in a friendly wave as I walked out the door.

I came back the next week at one o'clock, but, as I suspected, Charlie Laveur was out tending his traps. He had no more time for idle conversation. He was a busy man and he had given me all that he was going to give. The rest was up to me.

When Charlie Laveur showed me the bundle of the Eagle clan, my mind conjured images of the high-flying and powerful birds of prey. But the great bald eagle, from which the clan derives its name, has white feathers of wisdom on both its head and tail. It should not have surprised me to read in William Jones's ethnography that the raccoon is also a member of the Eagle clan. From his perch high in a tree, a raccoon has a farsightedness that animals like the fox and the wolf cannot match.

I read stories from other North American tribes that told how the raccoon came to make his home in the tree. In a Senecan story the Raccoon tricked the Fox into eating a "fire ball" — the root of a jack-in-the-pulpit. Then the Raccoon hid in a treetop while the Fox waited outside the Raccoon's former home under the ground. The Fox waited for hours outside the underground home before he finally discovered that his trickster was laughing at him from a perch high above. The angry Fox warned the Raccoon that he would get even, but the Raccoon yelled back that he would never be caught, for "no longer do I live in a hole in the ground like you. I live in a tree. Come on up!" The taunt angered the Fox even more, but neither the Fox nor the Wolf ever learned the secret of climbing trees and of living a dual life — high above the ground as well as on it.

Another famous story, told by many tribes, tells how the Raccoon tricked two blind men who were living by themselves apart from the camp of their people. He stole their food and watched as they fought, blaming one another. Then he led them to the river bank and laughed, revealing his identity. Finally he pushed both into the river, cleansing their eyes. Then they could see.

By now I was beginning to feel an intimacy with the tricky little raccoon, even though I could never seem to find one at home. On my first camping trip as a child, I had gotten up very early in the morning when the mist was still hovering around the grass, and I felt as if I were in the middle of a cloud. The sun was just struggling to come up behind the thick timber along the river bank. By myself, I walked down to the river to wash my face, and in the mud along the bank I saw tiny little handprints, with a thumb and five fingers. I pictured in my imagination a tiny breed of human being that lived perhaps under the ground or in a hollow log. With my eyes, I followed the tracks and there, standing on a limb overhanging the water, was a raccoon, unafraid and almost arrogant. He had a morsel of food in his hand and was washing it in the water while he held on to the limb with the other hand. He washed the food carefully, then put it in his mouth, ate it very slowly, and sauntered off. That was very early in the morning; I have seldom seen a raccoon in the daylight again.

On a more recent camping trip, Donna and I awoke to hear the garbage can outside our tent banging loudly. It was late at night, far too early for garbage pickup. By the time we could get out of the tent, the can was overturned on the ground and the raccoon was gone. Behind the car we could hear a high-pitched chattering noise; the raccoon was laughing at us. In the dark, we could not see. The next morning, we found claw marks on the outside of our Styrofoam ice chest and two choice pieces of meat were gone.

Friends who lived near our farmhouse told of vandals who repeatedly entered their garden at night, pulling off ears of sweet corn, taking one bite and leaving the rest behind. They soon learned that the vandals were raccoons, who will eat only the sweetest and ripest ears of corn — leaving the seconds for human beings.

Mesquakies believe that corn is a manitou or god. It has everything that people need to make them strong and help them to travel far. When we eat corn, the manitou in each kernel travels to every part of our body. Everyone in Iowa knows the value of good corn. The raccoon is particularly intimate with the moist yellow kernels. Our landlord told us that the only way to guard your sweet corn from raccoons is to pick it before it is fully ripe.

Often, late at night on country roads, my car lights have illuminated a raccoon, crossing rapidly to the middle of the road, then stopping, looking directly into the bright lights and blinking as if blinded. And often in the morning I have seen the dead body of a raccoon lying in the middle of the road. In the woods, however, there are no automobile lights and the raccoon has few equals in knowledge and intelligence.

A Menomini story explains how the nature of the raccoon was decided in the beginning:

> One time the Raccoon went into the woods to fast and dream. He dreamed that some one said to him, "When you awaken, you must paint your face and body with bands of black and white; that will be your own."
> When the Raccoon awoke, he went and painted himself as he had been told to do, and so we see him even at this day.

Some say he has a white face with a black mask. Others say he has a black face with a white mask. The raccoon stands in the dark shadows and laughs at those who cannot see.

One night last spring, I had my sleep halfway disturbed by the barking of our dogs. The dogs are stalwart guardians of our farmhouse, sitting near the porch steps or bounding after passing pickup trucks all day. Dogs have a close alliance with people that was established long ago in my culture as well as in that of the Mesquakies. Our dogs are strong and quick; they are good hunters and I have seen them outrace a rabbit or leap on the back of a ground hog, breaking the spine of the smaller creature then moving quickly to the kill, slowly savoring the prize for the rest of the afternoon.

During the day, the dogs have no equals around the house and barn, but at night they are fearful and they bark boldly but unconvincingly into the darkness whenever something they cannot see or understand threatens the welfare of their household, occasionally carrying on extended ideological disputes with the dog down the road. We have learned not to let the barking interrupt our sleep.

That night, however, the barking was louder and more frantic than usual and it lasted for many hours. I tossed and turned in the bed, not quite awake and not quite asleep. The barking had become part of my dream life, but it was a persistent irritation, and when daylight finally came, I was jerked to a complete waking state. Going to the window, I saw both dogs prancing excitedly around a fence pole, jumping forward and then back. Cornered against the fence, bracing itself against the post, was a raccoon. It was reared up on its hind legs, jabbing out with its front paws like a cat and warding off the dogs with a high-pitched growl. The raccoon was outflanked and was some distance from the nearest tree, but it had found the safest location, protected from the rear by the fence. It had been a very long night for all three creatures.

I rapped on the windowpane and the watchful dogs turned their attention for a split second toward the house. That split second was enough and the raccoon was gone — leaving the dogs bewildered and defeated, running around in nervous circles trying to find their lost prey.

24

I was gradually coming to know the important dates of Mesquakie history and the meaning of those dates in the minds of the people. What emerged was, for me, literature as well as history, for Mesquakies saw the events of the past as a coherent, unified story with foreshadowings and symbolic meanings. Their history was a story, but by no means a fiction. The events, dates, and places they talked about could be confirmed in the history books and documents of my culture. Truman Michelson said that Mesquakie history, told orally, conforms meticulously to non-Indian documents as far back as those documents go. My research convinced me that he was right. The Mesquakie memory is firm and does not alter events to satisfy egos. Rather it looks for and recognizes the sacred quality in those events.

One event, however, that Mesquakies of all ages talked about was barely mentioned in the historical documents. It happened around 1896 — a date that was mentioned again and again in conversations. The events of that year formed a story that was told to me, never in one piece, but in fragments. For Mesquakies, that year was an important beginning, a time when allegiances were made and broken. A person is to be trusted if he or she goes back to 1896. That year provided a cultural test, a time when Mesquakie values were seriously threatened by the outside culture. The conflict, like so many others in Mesquakie history, centered around education. The full story was to be found not in the library or the state historical society but in the Bureau of Indian Affairs Day School on the settlement.

I visited the day school in early February, on a cold frosty day. The large parking lot next to the school was nearly empty and it was a short walk from my warm car to the front door of the one-story white frame building. On the outside, it looked like an army barracks; on the inside, it was a typical elementary school. There was an unnatural hushed atmosphere that I knew would be harshly interrupted by recess. On a prominent wall inside the door was a bulletin board and the principal's office was nearby. The principal was busy that morning, but the receptionist was friendly and helpful. She ushered me into an office and handed me several bulging file folders of material. "You're welcome to sit here as long as you want and look at these," she said. "If you need copies, let me know." I sensed not even a hint of suspicion; she was used to academic visitors.

One of the folders contained mimeographed handouts from the BIA, giving sources of American Indian history or information about how to trace native American ancestry. One was a reprint of an article by Truman Michelson, quoting extensively from an older woman as to how Mesquakie children should be raised. All of the material was detailed, carefully documented, and useful. The secretary gave me one copy of each.

But the other folder was more interesting. It contained memos relating specifically to the problems of the day school. There was nothing private or secret, but as I thumbed through the folder I began to get a sense of the ongoing conflicts. None of the Mesquakies I had talked to had kind words about the school, but the folder reflected not an outright hostility but a positive concern for the direction and curriculum. There were notes from Mesquakies, clippings from newspapers, and research papers written by Mesquakies and outsiders.

In this folder was a research paper written by a young Mesquakie for a political science class at Iowa State University.

The Mesquakie student, admittedly a partisan Old Bear, was attempting to explain the meaning of the factional split on the settlement. This paper, together with the fragmented images and feelings that had been given to me in conversation, helped me piece together the story of 1896.

It seems that Maminwanige, the chief who led hundreds of Mesquakies back from Kansas in 1854, was an extremely conservative man who helped his people resist United States efforts to acculturate them. When the federal government finally recognized the existence of the Mesquakies in Iowa and agreed to resume payment of their annuities in 1865, Maminwanige continued to insist on retaining the old ways. When the government asked him to fill out forms listing names and ages of all members of the tribe, he refused. He could not in good conscience list the ages of his people according to the white man's concept of time and he could not so indiscriminately disclose details about the make-up of families. That was private and sacred information and even when annuities were withheld, he still refused to sign the forms. It was several years before satisfactory agreement was reached.

Maminwanige seemed to be accepted by all as a good chief, a man who protected the rights of his people and who maintained tribal harmony. But when he died in 1881, his son and heir, Moquibushito, was considered by the Mesquakie tribal council to be too young to take over as chief. Without serious dissent, the tribe accepted as chief a man named Pushetonequa, a member of the Brown Bear clan. (The chief was traditionally a Black Bear.) Pushetonequa was chief from 1881 until 1896 and, even though he was not strictly in the hereditary line, there were no serious disputes as to his right to be chief. The Mesquakies prospered as a people.

But in 1896, the United States government embarked on a policy that many Mesquakies considered a threat to their traditional way of life. Desiring to bring the Indians into the American melting pot, the government set up an "Indian Boarding

School" in the neighboring town of Toledo. The purpose was to teach children to get along in the white man's world. The first step was to take them away from their homes and families where the old ways were passed on through stories and traditions.

Mesquakies were almost unanimous in resisting this acculturation. The story goes that the schoolteacher stood outside the building every morning and rang the school bell. But no one came. Finally, after several months, four children enrolled, but most Mesquakies remained firm. Fifty years later, when the government attempted to shut down the settlement's day school and send all Mesquakie children to school in Tama, the same thing happened. Non-Indians called it a "school boycott," but on neither occasion were Mesquakies using an organized political method. When they see a threat, they don't need anyone to tell them what they should or should not do. Any organization that results is organic and spontaneous.

Finally, the federal government called Pushetonequa and three members of his council to Washington. Through the men of power, the government hoped to exercise control over the tribe. They offered Pushetonequa five hundred dollars per year and federal recognition of his right to be chief in exchange for enrolling his own children in the school. They knew that Mesquakies are likely to follow the example of a chief, but they did not really understand the source and nature of a chief's power.

Of course, Pushetonequa did not accept immediately. He went back to the settlement and thought seriously about the matter; a month later, he finally decided to enroll his children in the school. Pushetonequa's backers say that the decision was a sincere one, that he had become convinced of the value of learning the white man's tools. All Mesquakies today agree that those tools are essential to survival.

However, his opponents say that he betrayed his people and as a result could no longer be a rightful representative. A chief is a keeper of peace and order, a respected servant but not a delegated leader. Decisions are made not by majority vote but by unanimous consent. The conservative people ignored the government's recognition of Pushetonequa. They remembered well the time when Keokuk, the official government chief of the Sac and Fox, had signed away the land that they felt belonged to them by sacred right. These conservative people now put forth Moquibushito as the rightful hereditary chief.

Moquibushito's name means literally "Old Bear." The son of Pushetonequa, who served for many years as official government leader, was named Young Bear. Hence the names of the factions that have continued to struggle over the direction of the tribe. Because of the split, some members of the settlement have not spoken to each other for years. However, they are quick to point out, the matter is not based solely on name and heredity. "Why even the Old Bears are becoming Young Bears today," Mrs. Sturgeon told me. Even though the issues today may not be as clear cut, the factions not as neatly centered around family lines, the conflict goes on. It is a conflict over the amount of change that can be absorbed without destroying what is vital to the Mesquakie way of life.

The paper closed with an eloquent plea:

> The Mesquakies and their society have disclosed that social heritage is far more perduring than is commonly believed. Perhaps no other ethnic group has revealed this old important truth so convincingly as the Mesquakie has done. This capacity for perdurance is one of the truths on which the hope of our world rests — our world grown so pale in the last century and now so deathly pallid, through the totalitarian rule of some forms of government.

The word *perdurance*, repeated as it was, sprang to my attention. At first, I thought it was a misprint or an error. After all, I reasoned, the author was using English as a second language.

But when I looked it up in the dictionary, I discovered that the word was not only correct but powerfully appropriate to express the underlying theme of Mesquakie history. Built from the same stem as *endurance,* the word conveys the idea of lasting *through* a number of crises and changes.

As I thought about the word, I could see again the double image that had bothered me months earlier. I could see John Sturgeon standing behind a lectern quietly addressing a university audience; superimposed on that image was that of his younger brother, standing silent and alone near the timber with his shotgun and his World War I hat. They were both Old Bears and they were not about to give up the things important to their culture and religion. They were determined to perdure.

Before I left the schoolhouse that day, the principal arrived to introduce himself and offer his services. His handshake was firm and he did not at all look like the villain that I had expected. "If you have any suggestions as to how we can incorporate Mesquakie culture into the school, we'd sure like to hear about it," he said. His attitude didn't seem to square with the stories about him and the school that had been told to me by Lucille Waters and Isabel Sturgeon. Four months ago, I would have been delighted to find a warm, friendly face on the settlement. Now, however, I was uneasy and I retreated behind a nervous silence. I could not find words to answer him and soon the silence became embarrassing for both of us.

"Oh, well," he said, "if I can be of any help, please let me know." As he left to go to a meeting, he offered one suggestion: "Oh, by the way, have you talked with John Buffalo? He would be a good man for you to talk to."

25

Now I KNEW that I had to talk to John Buffalo. Most of the
Mesquakies I had talked to were members of the Old Bear faction. In a way, that was good — for Michelson had apparently
relied too heavily on the more acculturated Young Bears. But
I did not want to become too partisan and too closely identified
with one point of view. I wanted to understand the perspective
of the Young Bear faction and I felt that John Buffalo was the
most obvious and visible representative.

In late February, I finally made my way to Buffalo's house.
It was a bright day and the temperature had warmed suddenly,
but not enough to melt the heavy snow cover. The glaring sun
bounced threateningly off the piles of snow that lined both
sides of the road. Donna took the day off from classes and accompanied me on the trip. It was a pleasant outing and we
opened the car windows to help us preserve the illusion that
spring had truly arrived.

Today I was confident that I would hear many stories — so
confident that I brought with me the tape recorder that had
remained dormant in my closet for many months. James
North, who rode in the back seat, eyed the machine suspi-
ciously and was much quieter than usual. As he got out of the
car, he finally asked me: "Who's going to let you use *that?*"

"Oh, I don't know. I brought it along just in case." I didn't
let his quizzical expression bother me. I knew that any material recorded would be of marginal value.

John Buffalo's house was on the circular road that I had

traveled so many times the day I had searched for Charlie Laveur. It was a small house some distance from the road, and there were deep ruts under the slippery blanket of snow. Smoke was curling from the chinmey and the smell of burning wood was strong. It was a sure indication that John Buffalo was home from the hospital.

The door was heavy and very roughly carved out of planks. I knocked hard but only hurt my knuckles. I waited, then knocked again before there was any response. Finally, the door opened and John Buffalo blinked out at us. He was much older and thinner than I had imagined. He reminded me of the pictures I had seen of the classic American Indian, strong and stoic, with high cheekbones. He looked out the narrow crack of the door; I could see in his eyes neither acceptance nor rejection.

Finally, I spoke. "I'm looking for John Buffalo."

"Yes." His voice was thin and high-pitched.

I quickly introduced myself and Donna. "We're from the university in Iowa City and I'm interested in learning something about stories. I wonder if you'd be willing to help me."

Still that tentative silence — something I had not expected at the home of a member of the Young Bear faction. Finally he opened the door wider and invited us in. "Well, I'm not feeling well," he said. "But maybe we could talk for a short while." As we entered, I felt like a social worker — an emissary from the world that controlled hospitals, schools, annuities.

The house was even tinier than it had appeared from the outside and it was filled with native American artifacts — drums, paintings, beadwork. The bed in the center of the floor occupied nearly the whole house; as we sat in our straight chairs, we looked across the bed at John Buffalo, who sat in a straight chair on the far side of the room. The bed was made and everything in the tiny room was neatly in place.

My tape recorder became an embarrassing presence. "I have

a tape recorder with me — to help my memory," I said. "Do you mind if I use it?"

Again, that tentative silence. Then: "I suppose it is all right if you use it."

I decided not to use it and placed it on the floor beside me.

"So you are from Iowa City. I have many friends there." He was speaking in a slow, high-pitched voice. His intonation and his gestures were very formal. "Do you know Mr. Peterson of the state historical society?"

I did not know him.

"No? Well, you should look him up. He is the director of the historical society in Iowa City and he could give you a great deal of help."

On our many trips to the settlement, Donna and I had become used to the sound of the television or radio that was always in the background. But in John Buffalo's house there was neither TV nor radio and the silences seemed to reverberate around the walls of the tiny house. We were both more embarrassed than we had been since that first visit months before. I felt again that I needed the support of another person of my culture.

John Buffalo was giving us a lecture. "There are many theories about where Man was created. It is very interesting." He smiled and looked first at Donna and then at me.

John Buffalo was talking about beginnings, just as Albert Cloud, Henry Sturgeon, and Charles Laveur had done. "Some people talk about when Man first came to North America and how he got here. But some people say that Man was created right here. There are many theories." He was smiling and we had no trouble knowing which theory he accepted. His language was formal and he cited anthropological sources, but he was telling a familiar story. The Mesquakies were the very first people created and, as a result, they had a very special relationship with the creator and with the land on which we lived.

With the bed sitting awkwardly in the center of the room, his story seemed somehow less exotic, harder to accept.

My mind was wandering and for a few minutes John Buffalo talked with Donna about her studies in French literature. He was an erudite man, and he enjoyed talking about his years as a history instructor at Clarke College in Dubuque.

But very quickly he was back to his lecture on anthropology. "Do you know Dr. Sol Tax of the University of Chicago?" He did not wait for an answer. "If you talk to Dr. Sol Tax, you can learn about the social structure of the Mesquakie Indians." He smiled. "*I* gave him the information."

I had read Sol Tax, of course, and I understood John Buffalo's description, which was very condensed. Donna had not read the books, and I wondered if she could follow his brief explanation. "When a child is born, he becomes a member of one of two divisions. If the father is a member of one division, then the first child belongs to the opposite division. Then the second child will belong to the same division as the father and so on. So that everyone belongs to one division or the other."

I wanted to explain it further. According to the order of their birth, every Mesquakie, man or woman, is either a Tokana or a Kish-ko. A Tokana paints himself black with charcoal and a Kish-ko paints himself white with clay. They do this on ceremonial occasions and the two divisions carry on good-natured banter and are paired against each other in lacrosse games. They represent the two sides of human nature that are found in differing degrees in all of us. The Tokana goes straight ahead and completes anything he undertakes. It is a disgrace for a Tokana to die running from any enemy. But the Kish-ko is more paradoxical. A Kish-ko may give up if he pleases but is often known to win by trickery rather than straightforward aggressiveness. The raccoon, with stripes of black and white on his head and tail, is capable of being both Tokana and Kish-ko.

I was now beginning to wonder if the Old Bear and Young

Bear factional split was not a similar rivalry. For so many months, I had been led to believe that the differences were irreconcilable. The Young Bears were acculturated and pro-white. But were they really? Of course the feelings that I had heard expressed were real, but the differences between Old Bears and Young Bears were more apparent to Mesquakies than to me. Even John Buffalo, Christian though he was, knew his origin in the Red Earth. He too seemed to have the quality of perdurance. Was the factionalism a necessary tension to remind Mesquakies of the constant pulls that were on them, from within and without?

"What's the purpose of this division?" Donna asked.

"When games or contests take place, that is how sides are chosen," he said. "The first-born is on the side opposite his father and so on."

"What kind of games?" I asked.

"Tribal games." Mr. Buffalo smiled shyly. I had gone far enough with my questioning.

"Do they get angry at each other?" Donna asked.

"No, it is good-natured rivalry."

I remembered Michelson's statement that he had strong reason to believe that the dual division was used for ceremonial purposes as well as for tribal games. But Michelson was not sure and his tone implied that the matter involved an important ethnographic detail. I could not resist digging a bit deeper. "Is this dual division used at any other times? Or just for games?" I asked.

Of course, I was by now used to Mesquakie silence. I assumed that Mr. Buffalo was thinking about his answer. But after several minutes of silence, I decided that maybe he had not heard me. I repeated my question — trying to elaborate and explain. But again, silence.

Finally, Mr. Buffalo spoke: "It's nice weather we've been having, isn't it?"

Mr. Buffalo was very, very old and his house was extremely

small. I did not want to disturb him any longer. We thanked him for his help and left.

Several times in the weeks that followed, I stopped for brief chats with John Buffalo. But his health seemed to be declining rapidly and I did not feel I should disturb his rest for more than a few minutes at a time.

One day, in mid-March, Donna and I knocked again on the door of his cabin. As we waited for him to come to the door, we worried that maybe he had again entered the hospital. Finally, the door opened — just a crack. In the shadow of the door, his eyes looked very tired and his cheeks were even more sunken than they had been. His voice was high-pitched but soft. "I am very tired," he said. "Maybe you should come back another time." He was already moving away from the door as his voice trailed off.

Two weeks later, on a Friday morning just before I was leaving home for my regular trip to the settlement, I read in the Des Moines *Register* of John Buffalo's death. He died, we presumed, on that large bed in the very center of his tiny house.

26

JACK WOLFSKIN lived on flat land, just across the road from the Powwow grounds. In wet weather, the large clearing around his house tended to be marshy, but today a thick blanket of snow lay on all sides, broken only by the tracks of puppies who ran from under the house to bark at my heels, then ducked back under again.

The front door was permanently boarded up, and as I stomped the snow off my boots on the back step, Jack Wolfskin stuck his head out the door and welcomed me. He was in shirt sleeves but wore a heavy woolen cap, which he did not take off inside the house. "Don't worry about your shoes," he said, but I continued to stomp as I stepped inside. As I entered the kitchen, I could see a small living room directly to my right where a wood-burning stove was radiating warmth from the very center of the room. The smell reminded me of John Buffalo's house.

Jack Wolfskin was one of many artists on the Mesquakie settlement; I had several of his works on silk-screened tiles in my home. It was the peculiar power that I found in these works of art that led me to seek him out. On the kitchen table, his watercolor materials were spread out around a drawing board. Wolfskin pointed to the nearly completed drawing of a male Indian dancer. "A man from Des Moines commissioned a whole set of these," he said. Beside the drawing board was a transistor radio tuned to a rock and roll station — now blurting out news headlines. Jack Wolfskin shrugged. "When I keep at it, I can make a living," he said. He was a tall, thin man with a nervous smile.

His kitchen studio was obviously the center of his life, but he quickly put his work aside and ushered me into the living room, inviting me to sit down in a straight chair beside the warm stove. The radiating warmth and the strong smell of burning wood made me feel as if I were sitting around an open fire. This fire was crackling with much more liveliness than the fire in Charlie Laveur's wickiup. As I looked down, I could see the melting snow dripping off my boots in dark, muddy puddles on the linoleum. I tried to apologize. "Don't worry about that," he said with a laugh.

For a few minutes, we exchanged pleasantries, but Mr. Wolfskin seemed uneasy. Soon, he leaned forward on his knees and contemplated the fire in front of us. A long silence, then: "John Buffalo died last night," he said. Another long silence. "I believe you knew him," he added.

I nodded. "Yes, I did. I knew he had been sick for some time. But my wife and I were both very shocked and very sad to hear of his death." I could feel the sombre mood that Mr. Wolfskin had evoked sweeping over my body.

"I'm a member of his clan, so I'll be taking part in ceremonies for him."

"Oh, I'm sorry. I should come back another time." But he quickly motioned for me to remain in my seat.

The radio took over the silence that followed. When Mr. Wolfskin spoke, his voice was deliberate. "There will be a ghost feast, and as a member of his clan I will take part. There is a story connected with it. Maybe you know the story. It is about the first man who died."

I started to answer but Mr. Wolfskin did not give me time. In a slow, solemn voice he narrated the story and, as he talked, the radio faded into the background.

The first man died, and the people did not know what to do. He had died, and they couldn't understand. So they went out and fasted to find an answer. And after they fasted, most of them did not come up with an answer. But one man fasted and Wisaka appeared to him in a vision and told him this story.

The story was about the time Wisaka's own brother was killed by the manitous. That was the first time *anyone* had died. His brother had two names; one name was something like "kid" — I can't translate it — and then another name after he was dead.

Wisaka's brother was killed because he got separated from Wisaka. The spirits were jealous of both Wisaka and his brother because they were becoming too powerful. They were half-breeds, half-man and half-god. And they had powers that were greater than the powers of these spirits. The spirits were jealous and they decided to kill the brothers.

So they called in the boys' grandmother and asked her what they could do. And she said, "One of my grandsons has lived out almost the full cycle of his life. And there's nothing you can do about him. You will never be able to touch him. But the other one is young; he has yet a long time to live. About this one you can do something. You might be able to kill this one." That was Wisaka's brother that she was talking about.

So by trickery, the manitous got the two brothers out someplace. And they got them with two groups of people headed in opposite directions. And when they did this, the younger brother was killed.

And when Wisaka heard his brother calling for help, he jumped from hill to hill and mountain to mountain, following after his brother, trying to protect him. But it was too late. He was dead.

So Wisaka said that the others must die — all the spirits who had killed his brother. But the spirits did not want this to happen. They were afraid of Wisaka's power. So they told him that his brother could come back after four days. When we say that, sometimes it means four years, and that is what it means here.

So at the end of four days, his brother came back. And

Wisaka waited and he heard his brother come up outside the lodge. And he let his brother get only his fingernails inside the lodge. I guess that's because fingernails are the only part of you that will grow back. You cut off an arm, and it will not grow back, but if you cut off a fingernail, it will come back, just like it was before. So Wisaka let his brother get his fingernails inside the lodge, but no more. He was sad and he loved his brother, but he knew that was the way it was meant to be.

Mr. Wolfskin shifted his gaze from the fire and turned to look in my eyes. "There is a copy of that story in a book at the University of Iowa," he said. "I saw it once. It has the Indian version, in the old language, on one side with an English translation on the other." I knew the book; he had described it perfectly.

Jack Wolfskin's voice was high-pitched but evenly moderated as he continued. "You know we have to remember stories like that one. I will have to remember my part for John Buffalo's ceremonies. But at other times, we are not supposed to even think about the story. It is very hard, and we are supposed to get it right — word for word. The older people do it perfectly but some of the younger ones, like me, we have a rough time."

Jack Wolfskin was a man in his early fifties and the pictures of his teen-aged sons were lined up on the living room wall — an eagle feather above each. Jack Wolfskin was still a young man who had much to learn, much to experience.

I felt warm but at the same time awkward and embarrassed about the story he had shared with me. I felt unworthy of the honor. "Isn't that story . . ." I started to gesture but found myself unable even to find an adequate gesture. "Isn't it sacred?" I asked. He surely knew what I meant. He surely knew about Tom Youngman and Albert Cloud and James North. He surely knew that sacred stories were not to be told so readily to strangers.

Jack Wolfskin smiled shyly. "All of our stories are sacred," he said. "Some are more sacred than others." The sound of rock and roll music took over for a few minutes before he finished. "That story is all right for you to know."

In the library at Iowa City, I read the large volume of the Bureau of American Ethnology that contained texts, in Mesquakie and in English, concerning the Ghost Feast. Michelson had collected a number of versions, but I thumbed through until I found the one most closely resembling the one told to me by Jack Wolfskin. When I found it, I started in my seat and readers nearby turned to see what caused the sudden commotion. The English translation, collected almost sixty years earlier, had been written by John Buffalo. Although developed in fuller detail, it was exactly the story that Jack Wolfskin had narrated. As I read, I could hear the voice of John Buffalo, formal and eloquent, reciting:

> And so it seems, so be it, that the first mortal, so be it, would not learn anything from merely having a well-filled belly. The one who acted as a hero toward this Spirit of Fire, he was the one to continue to learn something. Oh, he got his knowledge from fasting. Yonder, it seems, after he plainly nearly starved his body so that he stumbled, he was blessed by our nephew, [Wisaka]. He was told by him, it seems, what happened to their lives. He was informed, it seems, how [our nephew] had been treated by his fellow manitous.

It concerned the same events, that first mortal who experienced death. But the archaic language, the indirection, made it a slightly different experience. It was harder for me to understand and I found myself reading it again and again. Yet it was easier for me to picture in my mind. I could see the Wolf stumbling along on his way to the river. And I could feel in my body the aching of that first mortal who gained knowledge of his body through fasting.

Through Wisaka, the teaching was given. It was a story of two brothers, perhaps the first pair of brothers. I could see

James North and his brother as children, running in and out of the tiny lodge where their grandmother lived. And I thought of my own brother, three years younger than me.

> After they finished eating, our nephews got ready. "We are ordered," people said among themselves as they came there. "Well, we are commanded from where the Great Manitou is to go about and look how the earth is and where the game animals stand," they were told. "We are brothers and we shall journey in both directions together according to the age we are, for of us brothers one [set] of us are Kickos and [the other] Tokans. The Tokans shall go in the northern direction and you who are Kickos shall look around in the southern direction and see how the earth is and where the game animals stand," it seems Wisaka and they were told.

James North had told me that Mesquakie stories are very condensed, and I knew that a great deal had been left out of this story that would be understood immediately by a Mesquakie audience. But what I was feeling now from the text did not come from the words on the page but from the formal, halting voice of John Buffalo. He was telling me about the dual division of the Mesquakie Indians. I could see Wisaka, the elder brother, face blackened with charcoal, walking toward the North; Yapata, the younger brother, face painted white with clay, walking toward the South. It was a ceremonial act that helped one understand what it meant to be a brother and a mortal. But without John Buffalo's voice the explanation was meaningless.

John Buffalo was sitting in his chair on the other side of that huge bed. He was silent and his face had little expression. Now, I could hear the voice of Wisaka punctuating the awkward silence:

> "Well, my uncles and aunts will pay close attention to the manitous at the time when they begin to lose sight of each

other," it seems our nephew thought. "And that is why we mortals each at some time meet death while we are living about with our fellow mortals at the time when it already has been fixed how long our life shall continue to endure."

And now four days had passed, and Wisaka could hear the sound of fingernails on his lodge door. It was a tiny lodge and John Buffalo was speaking the part of Yapata:

> "Now, Wisaka, they who have killed me have set me free, as you were so downcast in heart is why they released me. I am ever unable to open this, our door. Open it for me, my elder brother."

As I continued to read, the voice of John Buffalo merged with that of Jack Wolfskin and at times I could hear the lower-pitched voice of James North.

> Then it seems he was spoken to for the last time by his younger brother. "Oh ho, why are you so hard on our aunts and uncles? This is what would have happened to them: on the fourth day they would have come back, if you had opened [the door] for me, they would have come back to life," it seems he was told by his younger brother. "Well, my younger brother, I did not stop to think, that is why I did not know as I felt so downcast in heart when I lost sight of you."
>
> And we this very last generation of mortals, as many of us as are remembered [to be invited to the feast], we receive and eat this for them, likewise we shall fill ourselves with it so that we may reach an old age while mortals.

In the library, I found many versions of the story of the two brothers. Among the Menomini and the Ottawa, the younger brother is a White Wolf, chosen because he is the "smartest and fastest hunter." When he attempts to cross a lake on the ice, he is killed by water-frequenting manitous. The Wolf is fast but seems to be forever taking shortcuts. He is smart but does not heed his elder brother's advice to walk around the water.

The younger brother's name, Yapata, is said to mean "Wolf-like." He now lives in a different, perhaps a better, world in the West. It is the "Dancing Ground of the Dead," and whenever the drum is beaten, one of the mortals of this world crosses the river to rejoin his relatives.

Two weeks later, Jack Wolfskin finished the story that he had started that morning after John Buffalo's death. He told it as a separate story.

"Our stories are very similar to your religious stories," he said. "You know you have a story of the flood? Well, we also have a flood story. It happened just after Wisaka's younger brother was killed by the manitous." In the same soft, high-pitched voice, he told the story:

> Wisaka was so angry and so sorry about the death of his brother. And he killed some of the manitous that had killed his brother. And the manitous were angry and they sent the rain and it rained until the whole earth was flooded. And Wisaka was left floating in a canoe and there was nothing around him except water.
>
> And Wisaka sent several animals down in the water to look for land. And it was the Muskrat that succeeded. He brought back earth in his mouth and Wisaka took it and molded it with his hands and he created the world that we live on today.
>
> And he sent a bird to find some twigs, and he took those twigs and they became the trees. And he created the world as it is today and he created the people from the Red Earth.
>
> Then he went away to a home in the North. And he comes back every year and we can see him in the snow that falls.

Again, we were sitting in front of the squat stove in Jack Wolfskin's living room. A black puddle lay around my boots; outside, snow was falling in large, heavy flakes.

27

AFTER SIX MONTHS of traveling to the Mesquakie settlement, I had finally returned with a tangible artifact worthy of a collector of folklore. It was a story, an authentic Mesquakie story that could be traced in the *Motif-Index of Folk Literature.*

Harry Oster was elated. He was carrying his tape recorder and a briefcase bulging with books and papers when I met him near the mailboxes in the English Department office. "That's wonderful," he said. "Now that you have established trust and have a good informant, you will have no trouble at all." He was a small, busy man, a collector of antiques and stringed musical instruments. As he stood there with his briefcase, he looked like a chipmunk, his cheeks bulging with nuts.

He was a man who knew how to handle the powers of a tape recorder. He could get virtually anyone to speak, without fear, into the machine. As he fussed busily over the microphone, pressing buttons and turning knobs, the machine became an extension of his body, capturing the life of a performance. I feel sure that even Henry Sturgeon would have respected Oster's ability to use the tape recorder.

I did not have a tape of Jack Wolfskin's performance to give him, but that did not matter. Oster smiled shyly and hurried off down the hall with his briefcase and his tape machine. I was still shaking my head with uncertainty. I had established some kind of breakthrough, but not as a collector.

Some time ago, I had established trust among many Mesquakies — enough trust that they now felt free to joke with me and at times to tell me openly and directly what they could not and would not share with me. Their way was very different, and secrecy did not automatically mean distrust. One young woman told me that she covers up her beadwork when her sister walks into the room. "I don't know why," she said, laughing. "We're funny sometimes. I guess I don't want her to steal my designs." Then she quickly pointed out that none of the designs really belonged to her. "They are given by the spirits," she said. "Really, I don't know why I am so secretive."

The Mesquakies had many secrets — a full nest of food stored away for the winter. Many things I would never be told. "Why there are some things my own family does not know," Henry Sturgeon had said, spreading his arms wide and raising his voice slightly at the end of the sentence. His secrets were part of his body and I did not want to violate him with my questions.

Yet the story Jack Wolfskin had told me was sacred, and in my mind I could hear a militantly conservative man like John Waters saying, "Why, I wouldn't tell you that story for a million dollars." Yet Jack Wolkskin was himself conservative and he had been determined to tell me that story, even after I reminded him that it might be too sacred for an outsider's ears.

The process was not rational. A story so sacred that one man would not tell it was suddenly given to me by a man I knew only casually — just as Charlie Laveur had ushered me into his wickiup without waiting to hear who I was or what I wanted. "It sounds as if Mesquakies exercise a great deal of individual choice as to what they can and cannot tell," one of my friends suggested. But I knew that was not true. As John Sturgeon had pointed out on that first visit, "No one needs to be told what they can and cannot tell you. They *know*." There was an incredibly firm consensus about such matters — even among Young Bears like John Buffalo.

Because secrets had been hidden from me for so many

months, I had an unnatural hunger and thirst for such knowledge. I was like the hungry Wolf and the lusty Turtle.

Like the beadwork designs of the young woman and like the little dung balls of the Raccoon, secrets are personal possessions, to be owned and hidden away. But they are also gifts of the spirits and as such they are not truly useful until they are shared and expressed. The spirits are very generous and so are the Mesquakies. When the right time comes, that food which has been hidden away for the winter is to be shared and eaten. But Mesquakies know that the food of the manitous is not to be gained for the mere asking, nor by keeping one's mind concentrated on filling the belly. Knowledge and food are to be gained by fasting — by depriving oneself of the food that merely fills the belly and by forcing the body to feed off its own tissues. Only after one has fasted can the secrets be imparted.

Accounts of the benefits to be gained from fasting filled the pages of Michelson's books about the Mesquakies. At the age of puberty, a young person is sent to the woods to fast in search of a vision or a blessing from a manitou. It is said that an animal will stand up and speak plainly to the youth. Later in life, a person will fast usually for a specific purpose. Some people blacken their faces with charcoal and fast to prepare for telling stories.

I had fasted once myself, many years before. The hunger that I experienced was not the gnawing hunger that everyone experiences in the late afternoon. After a day of fasting, this hunger came from deep within the body. My muscles ached as if I had been doing strenuous exercises. A black friend of mine went to the woods and fasted for several days. He did not tell me what happened to him, but the experience was too powerful for him to handle. Very soon, he entered a mental hospital. Of course, there is a very real danger in fasting when one is not ready for the experiences it offers.

I had read Mesquakie stories about individuals who fasted overlong. One concerned a young man who fasted and was given a blessing. But his father told him to fast for two more days.

So in the morning when the old man went to take another look at his son, lo, the youth had disappeared from the place where he was staying! There was a spring at the brook nearby, and there the old man went. He went there to look over the bank, and behold! lying there on the flat of his belly, and drinking water, was his son. As he looked at him, lo, his son changed into a fish! He ran to his son to catch him, but his hold slipped and he lost his son.

Thereupon was the spring swollen with water, and the place where the young man escaped became a lake. For many years, it was common for the people, as they went canoeing about, to see catfishes down in the water. One catfish was white; it wore yellow earrings; that was the youth who had fasted overmuch. One catfish was black, and that was his wife. And there were also four other tiny little catfishes; they were all white, and they wore yellow earrings. These went swimming past side by side, abreast and in line, these the offspring of him that had fasted overlong.

There is much that fasting can teach, but that teaching can never be explained to someone else. It is an experience in which all of the artificial barriers between self and universe crumble. It is an experience that takes you ultimately to the water — where you can drink, swim, or drown. What one learns in a vision is private and secret, but the power that one gains is to be shared with those who are ready to use it.

I imagined that at this very minute Jack Wolfskin was fasting for a blessing similar to the one that was given to that first man many years ago. That experience I could not share, but I could share with him the experience and knowledge of John Buffalo, a mortal man. The story told to me was not a folk tale or a creation myth, related to life only through allegorical indirection. It was an event, as real as the person I had talked to behind the door of the tiny house.

Even though the story I had been told was one that was often included in religious ceremonies, it was no more and no less sacred than any of the other stories I had experienced on the Mesquakie settlement. The sacred stories that seemed so exotic and hidden were being given to me every time I drove down the roads of the Mesquakie settlement and talked to the mortals who lived there.

28

For the next several weeks, I spent many hours with Jack Wolfskin, questioning him about the story of the two brothers. We sat around the stove and, like a child, I asked him about matters that still puzzled me.

"Why didn't Wisaka let his brother back into the lodge?"

Mr. Wolfskin's answers were brief and not very specific. "I guess he thought it was better that way. And if you think about it, you can see that he was right. What would the world be like today if there was no death?"

"If the manitous were so powerful, how could Wisaka gain so much power over them?"

"Well, he was a special kind of person. He had the powers of the manitous. And he also had the powers that you and I have as mortal human beings." The answers were, of course, already given in the story itself. He seemed to be sending me back to the story for further study.

I read and reread the story, and I read many other stories about Wisaka that Jack Wolfskin did not tell me. Wisaka was a powerful creature who could avenge the death of his brother and who could unmercifully trick the Turtle for taunting him about his brother. But he was also at times a buffoon. He visited all of his animal brothers and he learned their powers. The Beaver sacrificed his youngest son for Wisaka's dinner, then brought the son back to life by throwing the bones into the water. But when Wisaka invited the Beaver to his house and tried the same trick, the bones splashed meaninglessly into the water. When Wisaka visited the Duck, his friend produced a tasty rice pudding by excreting into a kettle of boiling water. Again trying to imitate the power of his brother, Wisaka produced only his own excrement in the kettle. The Skunk turned around and fired shots, killing the Deer for supper, but Wisaka could only make a fool of himself by breaking wind.

Jack Wolfskin told me that these stories are intended, among other things, to teach children what they cannot do, as well as what they can. Each creature has its own powers and cannot assume the powers granted to others. As Wisaka traveled through life, he learned more and more about his uniqueness. As children hear these stories of Wisaka's travels, they learn who they are and how they are unique.

Only now did I begin to realize that I too had been traveling across the countryside for several months now, behaving in a totally disorderly and irrational manner. I was trying to assume powers that were not mine, to take stories that I was not yet ready for. I knew that I had been laughed at many times, even by a tiny mouse. They were calling me "Furry Face" and they were undoubtedly telling stories about me. But perhaps they were also learning from me, just as I was learning from them.

Jack Wolfskin knew that his answers could not satisfy my curiosity. "My father knows this much better than I do," he said. "He could maybe help you find the answers." Then he was quick to point out: "But he is in a nursing home, and he does not speak English very well."

29

Jᴀᴄᴋ Wᴏʟꜰꜱᴋɪɴ knew my culture well enough to want to help. He cautioned me that his religion was very important to him and that parts of it he could never share. But as a dancer, he shared with non-Indians "secular" versions of sacred dances. He seemed to understand that perhaps the same could be done with stories. He emphasized that there was much that he did not know and even more that he could never translate. He mentioned his father often, but I knew that his father, like Maxine Buffalo Robe, was not available.

As Jack Wolfskin talked to me, I could see, over his shoulder, the pictures of his sons. I could envision, twenty or thirty years in the future, one of those sons sitting before me in this very room. He would sit beside the same wood-burning stove and tell me solemnly that his father knew so much more — if only he were available to talk to me. Of course, fathers know many secrets and grandfathers know many more.

Jack Wolfskin told me stories about his childhood. Like many other Mesquakies, he had been forcibly taken from his home at the age of six and sent to an Indian boarding school in Kansas. He knew firsthand the story of the government's attempts to acculturate the Mesquakies and bring them into the American melting pot.

"I learned to fight there," he said with a laugh. "It was the only way to survive." As he looked at me, one eyebrow arched high into the air. It was a nervous mannerism that he repeated often. "But it was tough — being away from my family. To

Indians, you know, the family is very important." The long silence that followed gave a heavy punctuation to his statement. Finally, pointing to his drawing board in the kitchen, he continued. "I learned that in Santa Fe — a special school for Indian artists. They taught me the watercolor techniques and how to paint in the Indian style — without background." His art had brought him back home and had given him a way of making a living and of expressing his Mesquakie identity. "Someday," he said, "I would like to learn to paint fog in a picture. It's very important to a picture I want to paint and it can't be done with the traditional style." He was in a dreamy mood but not ready to tell me about the picture with the fog.

He talked more about his experiences at the boarding school, but his memories of life at home seemed more vivid. He always came back to these memories and to the stories that were told him by his father and his grandfather. "It was always in the winter, just like now," he said. "After the first snow has fallen, then the stories can be told. They are Winter Stories." Outside, the puppies were stumbling awkwardly through the heavy drifts of snow. Inside, it was very warm and the smell of burning wood filled the house. "Winter is a time of reflection. And it is a time when that person I told you about [Wisaka] visits us from the North."

I could see Mr. Wolfskin as a child, in a small bed pushed against the wall of a small room. He was listening respectfully as his white-haired father spoke in slow, measured periods of the oldest and most revered language. "Some of the words in the stories are very old, and we don't even use them today. But they are in the stories and you come to learn them through the stories. But they are almost impossible to translate.

"You know our language is not at all like yours. In our language, we can talk about something and never even mention it. But everybody knows what is meant. We understand from the context." As he talked about the past, the radio continually reminded us of the present. He did not seem to notice.

"My father would tell us stories at bedtime, and he would tell stories until we fell asleep. I remember some stories were very long and lasted almost the whole winter. And each night, he would ask us what we remembered from the night before and that is where he would start for that night.

"One of these long stories is about a man who had many adventures, but I can remember only one or two." He leaned forward in his chair.

> There was this young man who had a Magic Tablecloth. And every time he would spread it on the ground, it would produce all the food anyone could eat. It was a food supply.
> And as he was walking down the road, he met another man. And the young man spread out his tablecloth and they had all the food they wanted to eat.
> So the man liked that tablecloth and he asked, "What would you take for that tablecloth?" And he showed him the Magic Hat that he had. And when he threw down the hat, two warriors appeared. And when he threw it down again, two more warriors appeared.
> So they traded, and they walked off in opposite directions. And so the man threw down the magic hat and two warriors appeared, and he threw it down again and two more warriors appeared.
> And he said, "Go get that tablecloth."

Most of the story was recited in a monotone, but the final order, "Go get that tablecloth," was said with a great deal of animation, followed by a short laugh. Jack Wolfskin's eyebrow was lifted high in that winking mannerism. His smile was tentative; he wanted to see if I enjoyed the piece of trickery as much as he did.

I recognized the European motif. Some early settler may or may not have believed in magic hats and tablecloths, but his fairy tale had been transformed into an authentic Indian story. Now it was a Mesquakie story that was being given to someone who no longer understood the implications of the word *magic*.

To me, the magic of fairy tales was childhood fantasy, wish fulfillment, the charlatan who pulls rabbits out of hats. When I was eight years old, a magician brought me out of the audience to be his assistant. My heart pounded as I ran out on the stage; I could not believe that such a powerful man had chosen me to be his helper. But as I stood there beside him, I could see clearly what he was doing. I could see him pulling cards from his sleeves and pretending that they came from my ears. It was so obvious that I was shocked at the blindness of the audience.

Maybe that was why I felt a little uneasy at the trickster magician. I could see the white man, posing as a magician, using his army to take away the magic food supply of the naive and unsuspecting Indian. Now the white man had both power and food; the Indian had nothing.

Jack Wolfskin was still looking at me, probing to see if I understood his story. It was not until later that I discovered why. In a published Kickapoo version of the same story, the man originally with the Magic Hat is identified as a white man; the Man with the Magic Tablecloth is an Indian. In this story, it is the white man who is naive; he loses his magic powers by seeking an inexhaustible food supply he could have produced himself — through prudent use of his hat. He did not realize that, without the magic powers of the creator, all things are worthless.

The Mesquakies had used some of the money paid to them for all of their land in Iowa to buy back from farmers a small portion along the Iowa River. They knew how to use the powers of money as well as land to create new life. They had a Magic Hat and a Magic Tablecloth.

Now Jack Wolfskin was telling me another story about the magic trickster:

So the Man with the Magic Hat *and* the Magic Tablecloth walked along and pretty soon he came to a place and he married a woman and he lived there. And he was living in a manger, I guess, a stable. And they had everything they wanted to eat and everything was gold all over. It was like a palace.

So pretty soon, some men came and they saw what he had and they wanted to take it away from him. So on a hill near his house they brought a whole army of soldiers and as you looked out of the manger you could see soldiers stretched out in every direction.

So the Man threw his hat down and the two warriors appeared. And he threw the hat down again and again. And pretty soon there were warriors all over the place.

So the soldiers, they turned around and went home.

This time we laughed together. I could feel strongly the sense of security that comes from having magic. Mr. Wolfskin had told me only two small parts of a very long story, just as he had told me only parts of the story of Wisaka and his brother. He had apparently chosen for me the "secular" parts, the parts I could understand and share.

"It is very hard to translate our stories into English," he admitted again. "There are some things that just can't be translated." I knew of course that even if I did learn how to understand Mesquakie words, that would not be enough. Only a person who has lived through a tradition of shared experiences can hear those words that are left unstated.

I thought of the many battles that the Mesquakies had waged around that one-story schoolhouse. In an attempt to force acculturation, the government had cut the school from eight grades to six and finally to four. At each step, the Mesquakies quietly objected. But when the government finally said the school should be closed down, the Mesquakies no longer protested. They refused to send their children to school. The

Magic Hat was thrown down many times around the white frame school house and the United States government changed its mind.

Jack Wolfskin was telling me that the Mesquakies were the very first people created and that they will be the last people to be destroyed. "You know, we just want to practice our religion as we have been taught," he said. "And we are going to do it. And if anyone ever tries to destroy the Mesquakies, they will end only in destroying themselves."

"Do you mean the United States government?" I asked, shocked at the sudden expression of what seemed like militancy. But there was no anger in his face as he replied — only the passionate intensity and the shy smile that I had seen so many times. His eye was winking as he spoke. "No, I didn't say that," he replied. "I said, if *anyone* ever tries to destroy us, they will end only by destroying themselves. That is all. Our people were given that in a vision many years ago. That is what we believe."

There was a power in his quiet voice; I think it was magic.

30

Do you know the story of the Wolf and the Raccoon?" I asked Jack Wolfskin. He shook his head, so I told him the story as I remembered it. It was an old folklorist's trick that Harry Oster had taught me — a way of jogging the memory of a recalcitrant informant. If you make a mistake in telling *their* story, you might prompt them into telling you the correct version.

But the trick did not work. I soon realized that I was struggling to tell the story as fully and correctly as I could. It was as if I were on the stage before an audience of experts. I watched Jack Wolfskin's face closely but could detect no reaction. By the time I finished, I felt exhausted. But Mr. Wolfskin was still noncommittal. "No, I don't remember that story," he said.

"Do you know any stories about raccoons?"

"Oh, yes, we have many stories." He paused and leaned forward on his knees.

The Raccoon is always a tricky little guy. One day this Raccoon went down to the water because he was hungry. He was very hungry, so he goes down to the water and he lies down. He lies very, very still — doesn't move a muscle. It's as if he was dead; he pretends to be dead.

Pretty soon a Crab crawls out of the water and the Crab says, "Hey, this Raccoon is dead!"

So he goes down into his hole and calls all the other Crabs together and tells them that there is a dead Raccoon lying on the shore. So all these Crabs get out of the water and they are

so happy to see that the Raccoon is dead that they have a dance
all around him and all over his body. They're all ready to eat
the Raccoon who is lying there on the river bank. And they're
dancing around in a circle and the Raccoon is lying there very
still and he's just waiting till he gets enough of them so that he
can pounce down on them and have a dinner of Crabs.

But there's one Crab that's smart. And he notices an eyelid
winking. So this Crab gets around behind the Raccoon and
reaches out and bites his tail. And the Raccoon jumps up with
a loud yell and the Crabs all run away and get back in the water.

And the Raccoon doesn't get any food.

I laughed at the Raccoon loping away, his injured tail between
his legs. It was not often that the Raccoon is bested in trickery.
The Crab scurried backward — or was it forward? — down his
hole.

I did not know much about crabs. I had seen lobsters in res-
taurants, and in New Orleans I had eaten soft-shelled crabs —
crunching the legs and shell between my teeth as the waiter
advised me to do. Underneath the crusty shell I found moist
and tender white meat — some of the best I have ever tasted.
But the mere act of crunching the shell between my teeth provided a delightful experience. The Crab in this story is, of
course, the less exotic river variety, a crawfish or "crawdad."

The Crab seems to be an extremely ancient creature —
perhaps a relative of the dinosaur. Jack Wolfskin nodded his
agreement. "Our stories are very, very old," he said. "Many of
our stories have dinosaurs and other prehistoric animals."

The ancient family of Crabs laughed and sang joyfully as
they crawled out of their tiny hole along the river bank — that
hole that seems to dip dangerously deep into the earth, all the
way to the water. As they marched over the body of the Raccoon, some even convinced themselves that they had coura-
geously killed a long-time enemy. The dance was a victory
dance.

I have never really seen a Crawfish close up, but I can imagine that its dance would be very graceful — its legs and pincers groping out into the air. I have seen Mesquakie dancers at the Powwow who must have been dancing with a similar grace.

Jack Wolfskin was explaining to me about Crabs. "You know they have their skeleton on the outside. But they say that a Crab can grow back a whole leg if it gets bitten off."

"Just like we can grow back a fingernail?" I asked. Of course, I did not get an answer. The Crawfish danced his way backward with great speed, right down the gaping hole.

"And there is another story that is like that one," Jack Wolfskin said.

> One day, the Raccoon goes down to the edge of the water, and he lies down and is very still as if he is a log. He is hungry and he wants to get something to eat.
> And while the Raccoon is lying there, Ducks come along and crawl up on top of the log. And the Raccoon is just waiting for all of the Ducks to crawl up on top of him so that he can feast on them.
> But one Duck is a smart Duck. He is like the smart Crab. This Duck thinks that something is wrong. So he calls to the other Ducks, "Come on and let's start dancing backwards off this log." And they all started dancing backwards and the Raccoon could not catch them.
> And he lost his meal.

"That sounds like the same story," I said. "With different characters." Of course that type of variation was common in folklore.

But Mr. Wolfskin shook his head vigorously. "No, the stories are similar; but they are different stories. They have different characters and a different meaning." His eyebrow was raised sharply.

The story was a vivid picture in my head, but the ducks I saw

were the white Pekin variety that I had seen marching in formation along the Iowa River in Iowa City. When they swam,
they often formed a perfect arrowhead formation, but I knew
these white ducks were not native to North America. They
had been imported from China to Long Island in the late nineteenth century and had become highly domesticated, losing
their ability to fly. I tried to picture the more colorful native
ducks, but I could not. These birds lived a complete life — in
the air, on the water, and along the surface of the earth.

In all ducks the eyes are placed high on the head — above
the long, flat beak. Of course, a duck would not be able to see
anything on the ground less than two feet in front and would
be especially vulnerable to a raccoon disguised as a log. Just as
the crab looks down and back, the duck's eyes are pointed up
and straight ahead.

In Wisaka's travels across the countryside, he too tricked
some ducks. It was a well-known story that I had read in many
collections and anthologies. Pretending he had songs in the
bag he carried over his shoulder, Wisaka talked the birds into
dancing with their eyes closed so that he could tie their heads
together, strangle them by the neck, and cook them over the
fire. Together, the ducks danced, their closed eyes pointing to
the sky, swaying from side to side to Wiskaka's "song." For
Wisaka, it was an easy catch, but one duck (some say the Diver,
others say the Squaw Duck) opened her eyes in time to see the
danger. She and her followers escaped, but Wisaka gave them
bloodshot eyes for their disobedience.

"How can one duck be smarter than the others?" I asked.
"Aren't all ducks the same?" Ducks seem particularly instinc-
tive and group-oriented.

Jack Wolfskin was smiling shyly. I could not tell what he was
thinking and he did not give me a direct answer. He was a
dancer who traveled around the country performing for non-
Indian audiences. I had seen him, in ceremonial feathers and

leggings, and I had watched the flamboyant movements of the men and the mincing little side steps of the women. All of the dancers and singers took their cues from animals and birds. Each animal and bird has a power, a role in the harmony of the universe.

I knew skeptics who would laugh at Mr. Sturgeon's statement that "the answer is not in politics but in religion." These skeptics would watch Mr. Wolfskin's dance troupe as a fascinating throwback to a lost world. Dancing is a way of praying. And many dancers are blind — turning their eyes to the sky or bowing their heads meekly to the earth. But the man who understands the powers of the Magic Hat and the Magic Tablecloth is well aware of the danger of both these ways of dancing.

The stories were very similar; they danced together before my eyes.

31

ONE STORY in the published collections particularly intrigued me. It was a story about Wabasaiya or White Robe, a war chief during the early eighteenth century when the French and their allies were making war on the Mesquakies. White Robe was an historical figure, but his story is filled with fabulous events. No one would tell me the story, though I read it with fascination and awe.

White Robe was thought to be the son of an upper world manitou and from early childhood he displayed unusual powers. As a child, he was disobedient and abused other children. As a youth, he ignored his elders and went on war parties. To keep him peaceful, the Mesquakies made him a chief, but he continued to slay enemies, and he said, "I shall be chief and do this also." It is said that he dishonored the custom of hospitality to strangers — that he killed visiting strangers and gave their bodies to the dogs to eat.

Because White Robe exercised his powers so belligerently, war was made on the Mesquakies by other tribes. White Robe was a powerful warrior, but at a crucial point in the battle, he suddenly decided not to fight. He broke his bow over his knee and he continued to break the bows handed him by his people. With the same belligerence that he had displayed in battle, he allowed himself to be captured by the Peorias, who tortured him and burned him at the stake. As he was being killed, his supernatural power remained strong and I could strongly feel his resemblance to figures of my own culture, especially to

Jesus. The resemblance in feeling was there, but the contrast in rational content was strong and so shocking that I turned to the story again and again, trying to discover if White Robe was god or devil, hero or villain:

> Then White Robe was seized and bound with cords. "Are you hungry, White Robe?" he was asked.
> "Yes," he said.
> The flesh on his thigh was sliced away, and then roasted on a spit for him. When it was done cooking for him, "Eat, White Robe," he was told. After they had fed him it, "Are you hungry, White Robe?" he was asked.
> "Yes," he said.
> And then the flesh on the calves of his legs was sliced away and roasted on the spit for him. After they had finished cooking it for him, "Eat, White Robe," he was told. So wherever there was flesh upon him in turn was it sliced away and roasted for him. His own flesh thus he ate. After all his flesh had been carved away from him, then his bones were set on fire. When they were nearly all burned up, then an old man of the Fire-Nation appeared. "White Robe, you shall burn together with your town," he said.
> "Oh no, it is with your town that I shall burn," came forth words from the bones of White Robe.
> . . . Within the course of two years the people of the Fire-Nation were all slain by the Red-Earths.

The story was grotesque and powerful, but I could not decide how I should react. I wanted to hear it from a present-day Mesquakie who could perhaps help me resolve my doubts and questions. Was White Robe a scapegoat for the belligerent attitudes of his people? Or was he a savior who helped bring about the prophecy that the Mesquakies would be the very last people to be destroyed? What was the meaning of that grotesque ending in which White Robe eats of his own flesh until there is nothing left? Of course, the Last Supper could be con-

sidered equally grotesque by someone who had not accepted
the experience of the story, but the story of White Robe was
not part of my experience.

James North confirmed my suspicions that the story still cir-
culates on the Mesquakie settlement. "I read that story," he
said, pointing to the White Robe text in the William Jones
collection. "I asked my father about it and he recited it for me
almost word for word." But that's all he would tell me, and
when I asked Henry Sturgeon, Albert Cloud, and Charlie Laveur if they had heard of White Robe, they shook their heads.
Their faces were expressionless. Even Jack Wolfskin shook his
head when I brought up the name.

One Friday afternoon in early March, I was seated around
the warm stove with Jack Wolfskin and his wife. I had brought
with me one of the volumes of texts collected by Michelson for
the Smithsonian and the Wolfskins were examining the language, trying to help me learn to speak and read Mesquakie.
"This is very difficult," they agreed. "I can translate it," said
Mr. Wolfskin, "but the language is very old and it is not written
as we write it today. When my father writes us from the nursing home, he uses a different syllabary."

Together, they struggled over one particular word, trying
out different translations. "This must be . . . white? . . . I
don't know . . . maybe . . . white, uh, . . . white robe?"

Their translation was tentative and not meant for my ears,
but quickly I leaned forward in my chair. "What's that you
say? White Robe? Do you know about White Robe?"

"Yes, I think that is how you would say it." Mr. Wolfskin's
voice was calm and expressionless.

"Is that a story about him?"

"Yes, that is something that happened back at the time that I
was telling you about. When we were surrounded in Illinois.
It was back around seventeen thirty."

"I've been trying to learn something about White Robe for some time now," I said. Jack Wolfskin was looking closely at the text, his lips moving as he tried to reconstruct the story in his head. "Oh yes, I remember this. You wouldn't believe some of the things that happen in Indian stories." His eyebrow was arched.

Mr. Wolfskin knew that I was familiar with the printed story that he was reading and that I wanted him to tell me the story and talk about it. He deftly evaded me.

"You know that man was not just like you and me," he said. "They say he was different; he was part manitou." Mrs. Wolfskin was nodding her agreement. "You know back in those days, people had powers." He gave the last word an especially heavy emphasis. "They say that white people had powers once too, but they lost their powers when Jesus was crucified. Now white people don't have powers any more."

"When did Mesquakies lose their powers?"

"I don't know that. That hasn't been given to me yet."

He leaned forward in his chair, but the story he told me was not the one I was asking for. It was as if the mere mention of White Robe might invoke the presence of this powerful man. Instead Jack Wolfskin told a story that he had promised weeks before. I thought at the time he was changing the subject; I know now he was giving me the sequel to the story I had read.

It was back about the same time that White Robe lived; it happened in 1732 in Illinois when the Mesquakies were surrounded in the forest. We were surrounded on all sides by other Indian tribes and by the French and we couldn't get away.

There were two leaders. And they took the sacred bundle and started leading a song, a sacred song. And they drummed and they sang and they chanted until the other side all fell asleep.

We had two runners, what you might call messengers. We don't have them any longer. And these two runners took a sacred wolf skin down to the river. And they were supposed to drag it lightly across the river to produce a fog.

But I guess they got overanxious in their duty and they dipped it in the water, *dipped* it in so that it was all covered up with water. On the top of it: they *dunked* it in the water. I guess they wanted to be sure that it would work. But instead it produced too much fog — a lot of rain and a lot of moisture in the air.

So while these people were all sleeping, the Mesquakies were to crawl away through this fog. As we were crawling over these sleeping bodies, we were being led by these two men who had taught us how to get away. One man's name was Mamasa; he was the drummer who had helped put the enemy to sleep. And the other man's name, I can't remember.

But as our people were crawling over the sleeping bodies, the fog was so thick that we couldn't see each other. So in the middle of the line, somebody lost a hand hold and we couldn't see each other, so one group went in one direction and the other group went in the other direction.

And the other group got lost from us.

Jack Wolfskin's eyebrow was winking. "That's the story I have been promising to tell you. I think that story should be put in a painting, but I want to learn how to create the fog."

"Did the two groups of people ever find each other?" I asked.

"No, they never did. One group went west and we have never seen them again. Some people say they are the Crees, because the Crees tell the same story — except that they say the other group got lost from them."

The Rocky Boy Cree in Montana are an Algonquian people who, anthropologists believe, moved west many years ago. Lucy Sturgeon told me that they speak a language very similar to Mesquakie. "They know the real old language," she said. "They know some of the words we have forgotten."

"But what about White Robe?" I asked Jack Wolfskin. I

could not give up my compulsive desire to learn more about the man.

"That's like the robe or skin of an animal, a fox I believe," he said. "That's a story that happened just before the story of Mamasa." That was all he wanted to tell me.

As I drove past the Powwow grounds toward the highway that would take me to Iowa City, Mamasa's drum continued to beat. The beat was insistent, and I could hear the voices moving up and down the scale like the voices of all the birds and animals of the universe blending together in harmony.

White Robe was a Fox, a Renard. He was a war chief, the militant image that the French saw when they looked at the People of the Red Earth. But White Robe was a visionary who knew his destiny and that of his people. I could see his eyes glisten as he broke the bows across his knee and as he defiantly ate his own flesh. When government agents talk of the Fox Indians, they see White Robe and they see a vanishing race of determined redskins. They do not understand and sometimes they do not wish to understand the magic power of White Robe. They call it superstition.

But Mamasa was a different kind of chief. He was, I suspect, a member of the Bear clan. He was a drummer, a man in the center of the circle. His magic was not in the bow but in the sacred bundle. The sacred bundles of the Mesquakies are ancient and some say they were given to the people immediately after the Turtle forfeited his manitou power. The power that Mamasa knew is a perduring one. I had seen it hanging on the wall of Charlie Laveur's wickiup. I knew now the answer to my own question: the Mesquakies have not lost their supernatural powers. White Robe's body is gone, but he and Mamasa and all other Red Earth People live. Their powers are strong and if anyone ever tries to destroy them, that country or person will end only by destroying itself.

As an artist, Jack Wolfskin is still searching for a way to

create on paper the fog that was produced that night in Illinois in 1732. In his watercolor paintings, which are sold to white neighbors, he wants to express and make permanent his perduring identity. It is a story he apparently wants his neighbors to understand. It is hidden only from those who sleep and cannot see.

32

THE STORY OF MAMASA was not to be found in any published texts, but the events of the early eighteenth century were recorded somewhat accurately in historical documents. In the library, I had read "The Fox Indians Under the French Regime in Wisconsin," a publication of the Wisconsin State Historical Society. It is classified as a rare book that cannot be taken from the library and the pages are yellow and brittle with age. The story it tells is as vivid and real as Jack Wolfskin's wood-burning stove.

From their first meeting with the Renards, the French had been troubled by the Mesquakies. The French sought to set up a trading empire along the Mississippi and Wisconsin rivers from Canada to Louisiana. They formed alliances with many Indian tribes, but the Mesquakies were always belligerent. Whenever French traders, moving down the river, would see a torch placed on the shore, they knew that they were required to stop and pay toll to the dreaded "Renards." And the Jesuit missionaries, in nine years, did not manage a single convert among the quarrelsome Red Earth People.

There was no paranoia in Jack Wolfskin's assertion — echoed by many other Mesquakies — that the French had plotted to annihilate the tribe. At least four times, beginning in 1712 near Detroit, the French gathered allies from other tribes in an attempt to surround the Mesquakies and destroy them. Each time, the Red Earths were heavily outnumbered, yet through the help of weather (a fog, a rainstorm, a snowstorm) they managed to escape and survive.

The documents show that the final attempt came in 1732 in Illinois. That is the story that Jack Wolfskin remembers so vividly. The Mesquakies were surrounded for twenty-three days and on the twenty-third day, in heavy fog, they attempted to escape over the sleeping bodies of their enemy. An entire volume in the library — a dusty antiquarian tome entitled *Lost Maramech and the Earliest Chicago* — is devoted to a full description of this battle. It tells a tragic story of the lonely survivors of a once proud race. As the Mesquakies were crawling over the sleeping bodies of their enemy, their children, hungry and tired from the assault, began to cry. The enemy awoke, the story goes, killing all but fifty or sixty of the departing Mesquakies.

Hence, out of this historical event, there are two stories. One is a story of death and destruction, the other, of separation and rebirth.

For the return trip to Iowa City, I avoided the interstate highway that cuts so obscenely through the land and took instead the state highway that winds along the banks of the Iowa River. The trip is slower, but I was in no hurry. A light snow was falling, but it was late March and soon the ice of winter would melt into tiny rivulets and flow into the river. A tall line of timber guarded the bank, hiding the river but making its presence even more clearly felt. The river would be a good place to make a stand against your enemies.

The drum is still pounding steadily. I had heard it at the Mesquakie Powwows and I had heard it that first day at the Clouds's house. A steady, insistent heartbeat. "Some people pray with drums," said Mrs. Cloud. The drumsticks of her grandchildren had little furry tips, like pussy willows.

Around the drum sat the singers and around them were the dancers. James North was at the drum; I recognized him behind his sunglasses and his Western hat. And that little man, was it Albert Cloud? He had a high forehead and an almost Oriental look around the mouth. He too was wearing sunglasses, for it was a bright day in mid-August. There was a tall, thin man, sitting with his legs tightly crossed, his body almost motionless except for his mouth. And finally a very old man with tousled white hair and a white stubble of a beard. I knew it was not Charlie Laveur, but there was an unexplainable resemblance. Their heads were angled slightly upward and their dissonant voices were weaving in and out above the insistent, almost hypnotic, beating of the drum. "We do not dance to show off our costumes or to entertain the crowd," said John Sturgeon. "We dance to express to the creator our thankfulness for being alive."

Was it twenty-three days that the Red Earth People were surrounded with food? And when did they first start to beat the drum and sing? Was it at the very beginning or the very end? John Sturgeon was speaking: "In the beginning is the end, and in the end is the beginning." They were trapped in the timber, like White Robe tied to the stake. The French were there, providing military discipline for their Indian allies — the Kickapoo, the Illinois, the Menomini, the Sacs, and others. It is said that toward the end of the twenty-three days, some of the Sacs were sneaking through the lines to deliver food to the people trapped in the center. The military discipline was cracking, and the French were not sure which of their allies could still be trusted.

The historians speculated: perhaps the Sacs began to identify too closely with the plight of their former friends. And the French officers speculated: if the Sacs could be so easily won over, then how about the Menomini and the Illinois? All around them, the French saw Foxes. But victory was near, and that steady heartbeat that came from within signaled the last gasp of a dying race. Beside the tree, the French fell asleep — their eyes caked with matter.

The muffler of my car had once again come loose from the tail pipe and the engine gurgled noisily. James North would surely have a name for my car tonight. The historians could only speculate about the motives of the Sacs. The Sacs never told them why they entered the timber and joined their embattled friends. After that occasion, the tribes remained very close for more than 100 years.

I am sure it was a very old Mesquakie who told the story to William Jones of the creation of the Sac Indians. It came back to me as I drove along the Iowa River.

The People of the Red Earth dwelt a long time by the sea. Old men used to congregate at the shore, where they could sit and look out over the sea. On one of these occasions they beheld an object coming from afar, and making straight for the shore where they were. They watched, and saw that it was a huge fish. For a while its head reared above the water; and when it ducked beneath, up came the tail a-switching. Thus it came, first the head out of the water, and then the tail.

When the fish drew nigh, the people saw that its head was like the head of a man, and they were astonished. They watched it come to the shore, and when it arrived in water too shallow for swimming, it rose; and every part that lifted out of water became the same as a man. The tail was the last to change; it became legs and feet after leaving the water behind.

Behind the strange being came a great school of other fishes, and the same thing happened to them. They changed from fishes into people. They went up from the water and followed their leader. He was bigger and taller than all the rest. He was their chief. He led them off to a place close by the town. Everything they saw they copied. Everything they saw the Foxes do, they went and did the same.

The Foxes asked them who they were, why they left the sea, what manner of life they had while there. But the new folk were unable to tell. All they knew was, that they had lived in the sea, that one day they followed their chief inshore, and became transformed into people when they quit the water. Nothing more could they tell.

Thereupon, because they knew nought of themselves while in the sea, the Foxes named them Osagiwagi, which is "people who come out into the open." They gave the name as a symbol to show that they came out of one manner of life and entered into another which they knew nothing of before. It was a sign that they came out to become a race of people.

The Sacs are sometimes called "People of the Yellow Earth," but I think the meaning is the same. In the sign language, the name Sac is formed through reference to a shaved head, creating the idea of something sprouting up from the earth. Just as the chief of the Mesquakies comes from the Bear clan, the chief of the Sacs comes from the Fish clan.

Government treaties were made with the "Sac and Fox Indians" and that name still stands on the sign outside the day school. The two tribes speak a similar language and have similar ceremonies. Some of them intermarried. But both tribes knew they would always remain separate peoples. The same drumbeat that had drawn them together in 1732 would also keep them as separate individual entities.

The water was there in nearly every story. It was, as Mrs. Sturgeon put it, "the source of *all* life." In the water, all things were related. When Albert Cloud was a teen-ager he had been initiated into the icy flow of the Iowa River in mid-winter. He was telling it to Harry Oster, speaking into the microphone: "I was taught that all things are related — animals, birds, trees, even rocks. When I was a child, I was taught to welcome the seasons. And when the ice formed on the river, I was told to go break the ice and swim in the water."

I could feel the icy blackness tugging at my legs, pulling me down. My eyes were under the water, and I could not see. It was cold — so much colder than those late September dips in the swimming pool. It was colder than I could imagine and I knew that my legs would not be able to fight the icy current. Blood pounded in my ears.

I wanted to enter the water, just as I wanted to go to the woods and fast. But the experience of my friend who had fasted frightened me. I knew that in the woods and in the water there is a loneliness and a distance that is overwhelming. Yet there is, if one can find it, a manitou presence that makes all else seem like little pieces of dry bark thrown from high in a tree.

When the Sacs entered the woods, I am sure it was because they heard a voice the French could not hear; they saw a presence the French could not see. It was a voice that told them to come out into the open. I wondered if the Man with the Beard, so many years before, had heard a similar voice, urging him to travel west in search of the East.

Later that night, as I pulled onto the dark country road near our farmhouse, a small animal raced from the ditch and into the middle of the gravel road. I slowed down, waiting for it to cross, but instead it stopped directly in the middle of my path, as if challenging my noisy automobile. I came to a dead stop to avoid hitting the creature. In the middle of the road, the animal's mirror eyes reflected the light of my headlights — nearly blinding me in the glare. The animal refused to move. Gradually, I could make out the sharp outline of its body — the erect bushy tail, the dark mask around the eyes. It was a raccoon.

My unmuffled car engine gurgled and spluttered as we waited in the middle of the country road. Then, as quickly as he had come, the raccoon was gone. I continued home.

33

WINTER STORIES are to be told from the first snowfall of winter until the first frog croaks in the spring. That Mesquakie saying was repeated for me many times. In the fall, it sounded like a quaint proverbial expression; I did not take it seriously. But as winter melted into spring, I knew that it was useless to look for stories on the Mesquakie settlement.

I did not hear the first frog croak that spring, but I could smell the dark, moist soil as it came back to life. I continued to visit the people I had met, but they became harder and harder to find. The time for talking was past, and they were moving across the land. My visits became less frequent as I too got caught up in the movement.

Life that spring and summer was leisurely for us. Donna and I had no rigid class schedules to meet in Iowa City, and it seemed almost certain that there would be no job forthcoming in the fall. We spent nearly all of our time on the farm, planting a garden and watching it grow. As we crumbled the soil between our fingers, I could see the gesture of Charlie Laveur, explaining the process of creation. We took more than the top six inches, but we did not seem to disturb the magic that is in the soil. Our crops that year were fantastic; with careful canning and preserving, they would last us almost through the following winter.

I still had my dissertation to write, and I knew that until it was finished I would have no hope of finding a teaching job. But even that did not seem like a pressure. The more time I spent outdoors, the better I seemed to understand the events that had happened indoors the previous winter.

A raccoon tried to steal our sweet corn in August, but our dogs cornered it and killed it. Our dogs had matured considerably as hunters. After weeks of carrying around the carcass of the dead raccoon, our female dog abandoned it. And then, as if there were a cause-effect relationship, she came into heat for the first time. Our male and female dogs were good hunting companions but a terrible match. For nearly a month, they mated; again and again, we found them hooked together, crouching guiltily back-to-back and bottom-to-bottom and whining mournfully. They were sad-faced clowns and it was hard to believe they were the same dogs who had managed to trap and kill a raccoon.

In the fall, Donna and the boys returned to school and I spent hours by myself, looking over the ripe corn in the fields, trying to organize the material that was in my head. At times, I traveled to the library to do research on plants and animals. For days, I read about the habits of wolves, raccoons, crabs, and ducks. I did not see these animals every day, but then neither do Mesquakies see bear and buffalo. Animals who belong to the past exist as surely as those who live in the world of night.

The artichoke puzzled me. I could find nothing to indicate its use as a laxative — by the Mesquakies or by any other people. Yet when Wisaka boastfully ate the artichoke that sat in his path, he was soon overwhelmed by his own dung. What secret did this strange little thistle hold? My research in biology texts did not help, but one day, while reading a dream analysis by Sigmund Freud, I found an interesting reference to an artichoke:

> . . . My father, by way of a jest, once gave my elder sister and myself a book containing coloured plates . . . in order that we might destroy it . . . I was at the time five years old, and my sis-

ter less than three, and the picture of us two children blissfully tearing the book to pieces (I should add, like an artichoke, leaf by leaf) is almost the only one from this period of my life which has remained vivid in my memory.

He then explains that he developed in later life a particular fondness for collecting, possessing, and studying from books. In his dream thoughts, books were often connected with the infinite leaves of the artichoke.

The book pages that had piled up around me while I was researching the artichoke became for me part of my teaching. The artichoke is not a laxative, but its infinite structure can overwhelm. In Mesquakie, artichoke is literally "raw object" — one of a class of raw objects to be identified by its context in the story or sentence. Like Wisaka, I had to learn to digest my books and experiences before pouring them forth on the world.

As I lay in bed at night, thinking about the deer on Charlie Laveur's bench, I heard mice scurrying in the walls around me. They were trapped there, hidden house pets, and only at night, when all was quiet and dark, did they come to life like tiny hysterical muscles in the walls. I could see the pictures of the *Mus musculus* and its relatives in the encyclopedia, and I could see the tiny mouse dancing in Charlie Laveur's wickiup. When I was six years old, I awoke early one morning to see a mouse, its nose sniffing in the air for danger, sitting on the foot of my bed. Then it disappeared and I wondered if I had really seen it.

At night, our dogs would fight with skunks, and the pungent blasts of aggression would awaken us and linger in the air for days. Rabid skunks had been killed by our landlord, and we were suddenly seized with an overwhelming fear of rabies. In our 1926 edition of the *Brittanica*, we voraciously read about the symptoms of hydrophobia, "so called from the symptom of dread of water." The encyclopedia confirmed that the disease probably originated with the canine species, probably dogs and wolves. When a human is afflicted, he often goes to great lengths to deny that he has ever been bitten by a rabid dog. The patient gets extremely thirsty, but when he tries to drink, he is seized with a violent suffocative spasm and then an intense fear and distress, almost as if he were drowning.

I had naively assumed that the disease was now extinct, but we discovered a harsh reality. The odor of skunk lingered for weeks around the house, but our dogs had been inoculated and our fear of hydrophobia soon passed.

In December, with the temperature at twenty degrees below zero, eight furry puppies were born under the back porch. We could not reach them to bring them into the house, but they survived the cold and in a few weeks they ventured into the open — wading awkwardly in a heavy snow. Soon they were dipping their innocent noses into the bloody entrails of a freshly killed rabbit their parents had brought for them.

Through the winter, I wrote steadily. In the spring my dissertation was turned in and accepted. I knew of course that it was not finished, that I had come only a short way toward understanding stories that are as complex and vital as the forces of nature. It is a work that needs revision with each passing of the seasons.

In early June of that year, we took a family camping trip to Algonquin Provincial Park in Ontario, Canada. It is near the Saint Lawrence River valley, where hundreds of years ago the Mesquakies are thought to have lived and hunted.

Late at night, when the boys were asleep, Donna and I wandered down to the marshy shore of the lake where we could hear a very strange sound — almost like the honking of geese. It was very loud and as we reached the shore it became more clearly defined. We heard resonant vibrations, like the hum of a comb kazoo, blending together into a beautiful, ritualistic song. From all around us came the sounds, ranging up and down the scale, blending together in a call and response pattern. One was a deep bass; from our right came a twanging sound, almost like a stringed instrument, perhaps a sitar. And from far away came a gentle tinkling sound.

For minutes at a time there would be complete silence, interrupted only by the sound of waves gently lapping on the shore. Then one voice, usually the bass, would start off the chorus and soon all would be singing in harmony.

They were the voices of frogs and our flashlight picked them out from behind the reeds where they were crouching. A gentle mist rose from the water in the glare of the flashlight and the frog would freeze like a specimen in a museum. But from time to time we would catch a fat bullfrog in the act, his cheeks bulging back and forth with the vibration of his song.

As we walked back to our tent, we heard another camper remark, "It must be bedtime. There go the frogs."

The frogs were croaking in the spring. I thought of little Doe-Fawn lying on the Turtle's sacred bundle. "What do you want with stories? If you could not keep up this thing, then you had no business to get me started in the first place."

◊ 34 ◊

In April 1974, Donna and I traveled from Chicago, where we were then living, to Ames, Iowa, to participate in a four-day conference on "Iowa's Indians." A number of Mesquakies as well as other native Americans from Iowa and neighboring states were invited to participate.

My presentation opened the program. I was nervous as I stood in front of the large passive audience. It was my first opportunity to share orally my experiences on the Mesquakie settlement. I was uneasy about trying to express discursively the experiences I had encountered. I talked of what had brought me to the settlement and I tried to show how my expectations had changed.

> I expected to find a few narrative fragments of a dying culture; I found instead a living oral tradition that was functional in many important ways. Through the stories, people can relive important moments of the past; they can justify and explain social and religious beliefs; they can discover what it means to be a Mesquakie.

As I looked out over the audience, I spotted, in the back row, Henry and Isabel Sturgeon with the four-year-old grandson who lived with them. As I saw Mr. Sturgeon, I almost instinctively slowed my speaking voice and I immediately felt more relaxed.

> When I first came to the settlement, I said that I was looking for American Indian stories because I thought they were beau-

tiful stories. But I was quickly rebuffed. "If you are looking for beauty, then you should go elsewhere," I was told. "Our stories have a definite purpose; they are teaching stories."

It was John Sturgeon who had told me that. I now saw him in the audience with his wife, Lucy. They were sitting one chair away from John's parents.

> Through stories, children learn about the plants and animals around them; they learn how to find their way through the woods, how to fast and have visions, how to understand the possible and the impossible, the real and the fantastic. Through a story, a child learns the oldest and most beautiful words of a slowly evolving language; he or she can learn the history of the language as the stories of a shared history are told. And children learn discipline — the discipline of listening to a story and the discipline of living out a story. When a parent wants to caution a child not to be too proud or pushy, a story is more effective than a reprimand or an order. "Do you know what happened to Wisaka when he ate the artichoke?"

It seemed that Henry Sturgeon was listening with the same kind of discipline that he had expected of me. I hoped that my talk did not disappoint him.

> Some stories belong to certain people — a clan or a family. Some stories were not meant for me. The language, the culture, the method of storytelling are all very different from what I had been used to. But when we get past these barriers, we can find universal truths.

When I was finished, I went to talk to the Sturgeons. Henry Sturgeon's head ducked shyly to the side as he shook hands. His hand was very large and seemed to envelop mine.

The Mesquakies were involved in a court battle with the state of Iowa for hunting and fishing rights, and he had questions he wanted me to look up for him in the library. "Why, he's still writing with his left hand," he said, winking at Donna. Mr. Sturgeon's knowledge of the treaties, all more than 100 years old, was minute; I knew the information in the library would not be as accurate. "Yes," he said, "we know that. But it must be documented in the records before it can be accepted in court." Then he added, "You can help us with that, if you will."

Mrs. Sturgeon also had a question. "If you ever run across it, I would like to have the names of those people who stayed behind when the others were sent to Kansas," she said. "It is said that there were eighty *souls,* but it doesn't say who they were."

"But aren't there people on the settlement who know that from oral tradition?" I asked.

"Oh, yes. We have the information. I *know* my people were there; they never left. They lived near Cedar Rapids and runners were sent back and forth to Kansas." Her lips moved very precisely and she spoke excellent English. "But some of our young people today, they want to see the answers written down in black and white — even if it is in English." She had aged since I had seen her; the bone structure of her face was sharp and unequivocal. In her quiet way, she was extremely proud. "And if that is what our young people want, I think that we should give it to them."

I had brought with me a copy of my dissertation and I gave it to John Sturgeon for the tribal Education Committee. He seemed delighted. "As I told you earlier, this will be very helpful to us when we get our bilingual and bicultural school," he said. He was taller than I had remembered but not as harsh or as intimidating as he had seemed to me that first day. His manner was very much like that of his mother — precise and proud yet gentle.

I was embarrassed as he thumbed through the awkward bulk of paper that I had put together so laboriously. It was over

400 pages, including footnotes and bibliography. Some of my professors had thought it not quite as scholarly as it should have been for a dissertation; now I knew it was far too scholarly. "I'm sure there are many mistakes," I said. "I'd really like to have some reactions from the tribe — both positive and negative."

John shrugged. "Of course, it is a white perspective. If we put it together with an Indian perspective — then we will really have something." He tapped the bulk of paper with his fingers. "This is important. I can see already the criticism will be mostly positive."

The Sturgeons stayed for the entire conference, and we saw them again and again at seminars and at faculty receptions. As always, they were quiet and nondemonstrative but comfortable and at ease. As they told us about their activities, on the settlement and in the community, Donna and I could see how totally involved they were in keeping their culture alive and in forming the kinds of ties with the outside world that allowed them to continue their old ways. Both John and his mother had been to Washington, D.C., a number of times to push their case for the bilingual, bicultural school on the settlement, kindergarten through eighth grade. They assured me that the school would be a reality. Red brick — invulnerable.

The Sturgeons were staunchly traditional, yet they now knew that certain bridges to the outside world were essential.

On Saturday morning, there was a panel discussion involving native Americans from Iowa, Nebraska, and South Dakota. John Sturgeon and his mother were on the panel and were joined by Jack Wolfskin, who drove up for the day.

As John stood at the podium, he held in front of him my awkward bundle of paper. I wanted to disappear, but I felt the tiny little mouse dancing around me. John's hair was in a modern, semilong style and he seemed almost Oriental. He was holding my dissertation in his hands, pointing to it, and telling the audience essentially what he had told me two days earlier. It was an important thing to do, and he publicly thanked me.

John then told the audience how the government had for years tried to discourage Mesquakies from speaking their language and learning their stories and traditions. "We have to fight to maintain that culture that makes us Indians," he said. Then he paused for several seconds and I could sense that he was preparing to launch into the flowery eloquence that was so natural for him. But first he apologized. "My wife told me this morning, 'Don't be too windy.' So I will try not to be too windy. But maybe that is my nature." He waited again, for dramatic impact. "I just want to say that there are beginnings and there are ends. Where there is a beginning, there is an end. When we have found an end, then we must seek for a beginning." He walked back to his seat.

Isabel Sturgeon continued along the same line that her son had started. She talked about the school building that had been promised them:

> We want a school building for our children. That is in the records and I won't go into it any further. The next thing that I would ask is that they have a room for our Indian language classes that we have started and that we be allowed to teach language and other parts of our culture in that school.
> If our young people want something, we should give them the answers that they want. If they want to see things written down, then that is what we should give them — even if it is in your language.

Several years ago, I would have interpreted her speech as an indication that acculturation was rapidly wiping out the Mesquakie language and culture. That is what Truman Michelson understood in 1916 and it was what some anthropologists felt in the 1950s. Changes were taking place on the settlement, as always, and Mesquakies were the first to recognize those changes and sometimes to complain about them. But the fact that Mesquakies saw a need for language classes was not necessarily an indication that the language was being lost. The very complaint was like an exercise in perdurance. I knew that James North would become Jack Wolfskin; Jack Wolfskin would become Henry Sturgeon; Henry Sturgeon would become Charlie Laveur. Young people would grow old and would complain about the young people who were changing from the old ways. Young people always pose a threat to a traditional culture; they are always tempted to turn it over in the face of changing conditions in the outside world. But the beat of the drum on the inside of the circle, that was what was important. I could see James North at the drum, singing. I knew that Mrs. Sturgeon had no doubt that the traditional oral culture of the Mesquakies would continue.

In one of the books I had read, there was a quote from an older Mesquakie, given to Truman Michelson:

> There is, in a way, a story that when an Indian dies, he really doesn't die. He merely wanders on this earth. When it is said, "He is dead," he really is not. He is merely absent for a while. Soon he will be seen, and all will see each other again. That is one thing those who know tell. That is why some of those who know do not feel badly when anyone dies. Oh, the younger people, to be sure, do not know this story. That is why they feel very badly when they lose sight of their relatives.

Now Jack Wolfskin was speaking, his voice choked with emotion:

> Today, I have obligations on the settlement; I am supposed to be there. I am hoping that my grandfathers will forgive me for what I am doing today. But I thought it would be better for me to be here.
>
> I want to let you know what it means to be an Indian and to let you know what I have seen in my lifetime. The Indian

today is moving forward to try to help the white man understand. From what I have seen, your culture is altogether different.

We have always stressed education. And we are trying to
learn your language so we can understand you because you are
not learning our language so you can understand us.

One thing you cannot do is join our religion. Why should
you leave the religion you have had all your lives? Each individual tribe was given its own particular religion to practice as
they saw fit. That is what is most important to us.

We are more religious than any race I know of. It is not just
on Sunday, but we are aware of our religion on every day in everything that we do.

I am sure that my tribe will succeed and that they will all
unite. You cannot join our religion, but if you could, you
would have to learn many things.

Perhaps through Powwows, we can help people understand.
These are my people. I believe in what they are doing. Maybe
one day, people will know.

He paused at the podium, one eyebrow arched. Then he
walked back to his place.

The final event of the four-day conference was a Powwow.
Jack Wolfskin had to return to the settlement before the dancing began, but I could see him on the gymnasium floor in ceremonial dress. As the drum beat, I could see the fog rise from
the river and I could see a People walking hand in hand over
sleeping bodies.

The final dance was the Friendship Dance, and John
Sturgeon, from his microphone on the stage, explained that all
guests and visitors were invited to take part as a symbol of
friendship. The tone of the dance was not as intense — a
steady beat and a one-two side step. Over the microphone,
John Sturgeon tried to teach the awkward and self-conscious

non-Indians. "One-two, step. That's it." And very soon, it was comfortable.

In the center of the circle were the drummers. James North was there, his attention fixed intensely on the drum and the area immediately above it. We had talked with him briefly just before the dance, and he had introduced us to his new wife. She was very young.

"Are you still at Iowa?"

"No, I've enrolled at North Dakota for next year. One more try, Freddy."

It was too far from home; I suspected it would last no more than one semester. But his education was no problem; he would someday be as old as Maxine Buffalo Robe.

The other drummers I did not recognize, but one short man in sunglasses reminded me of Albert Cloud. The white-haired man with the stubble of beard looked like Charlie Laveur. The resemblance in each case was not rational — based on vague, unverified feelings. Their voices blended smoothly above the steady beat of the drum.

Around the circle, we followed our leader, a very large, smiling man. His belly protruded beneath his beaded vest. He swung his elbows in a sweeping arc as he moved around the circle, as if he were lifting his heavy body from the ground. Then he would soar gracefully in the breeze, like a majestic bald eagle. He would turn periodically to those of us following in his trail and he would smile broadly. The one-two step soon became natural and I could feel my body taking over, moving by itself to the beat of the Powwow drum.

Guide to Further Reading

Blair, Emma Helen. *The Indian Tribes of the Upper Mississippi Valley and Region of the Great Lakes.* Cleveland: The Arthur H. Clark Co., 1912. Accounts of Central Woodlands Indian tribes by early French and American explorers and army officers.

Busby, Allie B. *Two Summers Among the Mesquakies.* Vinton, Iowa: Herald Book and Job Room, 1886. An account of a missionary who lived among the Mesquakies in Iowa.

Fulton, A. R. *The Red Men of Iowa.* Des Moines, 1882.

Gearing, Frederick. *The Face of the Fox.* Chicago: Aldine Publishing Co., 1970.

Gearing, Frederick; Netting, Robert McC.; and Peattie, Lisa R. *Documentary History of the Fox Project: 1948–1959.* Chicago: Department of Anthropology, University of Chicago, 1960. A collection of letters and other documents relating to the activities of those engaged in "action anthropology" at the Mesquakie settlement.

Hagan, William T. *The Sac and Fox Indians.* Norman: University of Oklahoma Press, 1958. Pertains mostly to the Sacs and Mesquakies who remained in Kansas and now live in Oklahoma.

Jacobs, Melville. *The Content and Style of an Oral Literature.* Viking Fund Publications in Anthropology No. 26. New York, 1959. An argument in favor of studying the context as well as the text of American Indian stories.

Jones, William. "The Algonkin Manitou." *Journal of American Folklore,* 18 (1905), 183–190.

———. "Episodes in the Culture-Hero Myth of the Sauks and Foxes." *Journal of American Folklore,* 15 (1901), 225–239.

———. *Ethnography of the Fox Indians,* ed. Margaret Welpley Fisher.

Bureau of American Ethnology, Bulletin 125. Washington: U.S. Government Printing Office, 1938. The fullest and most reliable anthropological account, compiled in 1901 and 1902.

———. *Fox Texts.* Publications of the American Ethnological Society, Vol. 1. Leyden, 1907.

———. "Notes on the Fox Indians." *Journal of American Folklore,* 24 (1911), 209–237.

Jones, William, and Michelson, Truman. *Kickapoo Tales.* Publications of the American Ethnological Society, Vol. 9. Leyden, 1915. A collection of stories from a closely related tribe. A full version of "The Man with the Magic Tablecloth" story is included.

———. *Ojibwa Texts.* 2 vols. Publications of the American Ethnological Society, Vol. 7, Parts 1 and 2. Leyden, 1907. The style of Ojibwa stories is vastly different, the content often similar to that of the Mesquakies.

Kellogg, Louise P. "The Fox Indians During the French Regime." Wisconsin State Historical Society Proceedings, 55 (1907), 142–188. An excellent source of Mesquakie history, especially during the period of White Robe and Mamasa.

Lasley, Mary. "Sac and Fox Tales." *Journal of American Folklore,* 15 (1902), 170–178. Mrs. Lasley is a Sac and Fox who remained in Kansas. She also tells a version of the Mamasa story.

Michelson, Truman. "How Meskwaki Children Should Be Brought Up." In *American Indian Life,* ed. Dr. Elsie Clews Parsons, pp. 81–86. New York, 1922.

———. *Notes on Fox Mortuary Customs and Beliefs.* Fortieth Annual Report of the Bureau of American Ethnology. Washington: U.S. Government Printing Office, 1925. Contains bibliography on mortuary customs and beliefs and eleven texts concerning what is to be done when a Mesquakie dies.

———. "A Select Fox Bibliography." In *Mythical Origin of the White Buffalo Dance of the Fox Indians.* Fortieth Annual Report of the Bureau of American Ethnology. Washington: U.S. Government Printing Office, 1925. At least 31 other articles or monographs by Michelson about the Mesquakies can be found, mostly in publications of the Bureau of American Ethnology.

Owen, Mary Alicia. *Folk-Lore of the Mesquakie Indians of North America.*

London: David Nutt, 1904. Labeled unreliable and inauthentic by Truman Michelson.

Radin, Paul. *Literary Aspects of North American Mythology.* Anthropology Series of the Canada Geological Survey, No. 6, Museum Bulletin No. 16. Ottawa, 1915.

———. *The Trickster.* New York: Bell Publishing Co., 1956. Also Schocken paperback, 1971. The fullest and most readily available collection of Central Woodlands trickster stories.

Rideout, Henry Milner. *William Jones.* New York: Frederick A. Stokes Co., 1912. A biography of the part-Mesquakie anthropologist who compiled *Fox Texts.*

Skinner, Alanson, and Saterlee, John V. *Folklore of the Menomini Indians.* The American Museum of Natural History, Anthropological Papers, Vol. 13, Part 3, pp. 217–546. New York, 1915.

Smith, Huron H. *Ethnobotany of the Meskwaki Indians.* Milwaukee Public Museum Bulletin, Vol. 4, No. 2. Milwaukee, 1928. Smith also compiled ethnobotanies of the Menomini and Ojibwa Indians, published in the Milwaukee Museum Bulletin.

Steward, J. F. *Lost Maramech and Earliest Chicago.* Chicago: Fleming H. Revell Co., 1903. An antiquarian account of the battle of 1732.

Tax, Sol. "The Social Organization of the Fox Indians." In *Social Anthropology of North American Tribes,* ed. Fred Eggan. Chicago: The University of Chicago Press, 1937.

Wanatee, Donald W. "The Lion, the Fleur de Lis, the Eagle, or the Fox: A Study of Government." Unpublished paper written by a former member of the Mesquakie Tribal Council. Copies available at the Bureau of Indian Affairs office, Sac and Fox Area Day School, Tama settlement.

Waseskuk, Bertha. "Mesquakie History — As We Know It." Published in official program for 51st anniversary Mesquakie Indian Powwow, August 1966.

Index

Acculturation: 27, 33, 39, 131, 132, 156, 160, 189; *see also* boarding school

Animal stories: 37; humor in, 39; purpose of, 39; *see also* stories, Mesquakie

Anthropologists: 4, 6, 10, 13, 14, 22, 36

Anthropology: 6, 14, 16

Artichoke: 181-82

Artists, Mesquakie: 12, 15, 17, 27, 29, 93, 94, 141-42, 157, 171; *see also* North, James; Wolfskin, Jack; Youngman, James

Bear: 84

Bear clan, 172; Black and Brown Bear clans, 131

Bilingual, bicultural school: 57, 188, 189

Black Elk Speaks (John Neihardt): 5, 34, 43

Black Hawk: 9, 11, 61

Black Hawk War: 11, 61

Boarding school as means of acculturation: 132, 156

Buffalo, John: 25, 27, 28, 38, 41, 134-40, 142, 145-48, 152

Buffalo Robe, Maxine: 93, 102

Bundles, sacred: 37, 85-88, 121, 171-72

"Center of island": 62, 108, 110

Christianity and Mesquakie culture: 25, 27, 28, 58, 167-68; *see also* religion, white

Clan names: 35; Bear, 172; Black Bear, 131; Brown Bear, 131; Eagle, 42, 121, 124; Fish, 35, 178; Fox, 112; Thunder, 35; War Chief, 121

Clearings in woods: 56, 105, 108

Cloud, Albert: 6, 7, 11, 12, 15, 17, 18, 20-24, 176, 192

Cloud, Raymond: 22-24

Cloud, Ruth: 12, 15, 18, 19, 20-24

Continuity through change: 102; *see also* perdurance

Corn: 8, 61, 92, 106, 111, 113; as a manitou, 126

Crab: 162-64

Creation: 111-12, 137, 148, 161

Dancing: 164, 165; as expression of friendship, 191-92; as religious experience, 156

Darwin's theory of evolution, Mesquakie view: 92

Death, Mesquakie customs relating to: 113, 142; feigned death, 162-63; ghost feast, 143-45; death as necessity, 154; death as separation, 143-44

Deer: 75-77, 79, 114-22, 182; powers of, 116

"Discovery" America: 64, 105-108, 110

Disorientation: 46-48, 105, 111, 121

Doe-Fawn: 85, 89, 184

Dogs: 35, 36, 109, 115, 127, 128, 141, 181

Doors: 11, 141

Drumming: 6, 15, 17, 148; used for

praying, 175–76
Duck: 164–66

Eagle: 117, 124, 192
Eagle clan: 42, 121, 124
Eating or hunger as search: 26, 27, 31, 44–49, 65, 66, 68, 72, 81, 98, 111, 151, 162
Eloquence of Mesquakies: 111
Ethnographic data: 31

Factional split among Mesquakies: 133, 138
Fasting: 19, 143, 145, 151–52
Fire: 45, 118
Fish: 152; becomes a man, 177
Fish clan: 35, 178
Flood, story of: 148
Fog: see mist
Folk beliefs, Mesquakie: 98, 116, 117, 119
Folk beliefs, non-Mesquakie: 6, 8, 9, 21
Folklore, collecting: 1, 4, 6, 126, 30, 149, 162
Food: 111, 113; see also eating or hunger as search
Four as a sacred number: 51, 52, 58, 65, 66, 68
Fox: 10, 172
Fox clan: 112; name mistaken for name of tribe, 112
"Fox Indians Under the French Regime in Wisconsin" (Wisconsin State Historical Society): 174
Fox Tests (William Jones): 42, 84, 101, 103
French relationship with Mesquakies: 174–75
Frogs: 180, 184
Future, seen in past: 51, 62, 110

Gearing, Fred: 6, 13, 22, 23
Genealogy "ledger": 65–66
Generosity of Mesquakies: 28, 45, 151

Ghost Feast: 143–45
Grandmother: 85; earth as, 113, 114

He-Who-Lies-With-Eyes-Bulging-Through-the-Smoke-Hole: 118
History, Mesquakie concept of: 60–64; oral history, 129; and stories, 62; as a unified story, 129; as a visionary quest, 63–64; as vision of future, 51, 62, 110
Hospitality, Mesquakie: 58, 167
Houses, very small: John Buffalo's, 135–40; Maxine Buffalo Robe's, 11, 101, 102; Tom Youngman, 99
Hunters: 56–59, 117–18

Indirection of Mesquakies: 37, 50
Iowa: as a special place, 7; land, 8; weather, 21, 26, 67, 84, 105, 124, 134
Iowa River: 9, 82, 106, 122, 123, 147, 175–79
Iowa, University of: 4, 5, 54, 82, 149

Jones, William: 13, 42, 78, 112; see also Fox Texts
Joseph, Chief: 9

Kansas, reservation in: 61
Keokuk: 9, 11, 61, 133
Kish-ko: 138

Land use, Mesquakie: 2, 7, 9; burial and farming and top six inches, 112–13, 180; importance of land, 62; ownership of land, 113; a special place, 108
Language, English: 11, 15
Language, Mesquakie: 11, 15, 16; changes, 23; context and reference, 23, 157; difficulty of translation, 95–96; "given" to Mesquakies, 96; learned through stories, 157; written syllabary, 169
Laveur, Charlie: 105, 108–24, 150, 176, 182; sister of, 108
Lodges, Mesquakie: 9, 10, 26, 108,

109, 115, 118, 123
Lost Maramech and the Earliest Chicago (J. F. Steward): 175

Magic powers, loss of: 170–71
Mamasa: 171–72, 174–75
Maminwanige: 131
"Man with beard": 2, 29, 51–52, 65, 71, 97, 108, 110, 124, 155, 179; *see also* stories, Mesquakie
Manitous: 122, 143–48, 154–55, 170
Menstrual lodge: 85, 120
Mesquakie Day School: 10, 15, 16, 102, 130
Mesquakie Indian Boarding School, Toledo, Ohio: 132
Mesquakies of Iowa, The: 14
Michelson, Truman: 14, 36, 37, 41, 78, 107, 129, 130, 139, 194
Mink: 48
Mist (fog): 125, 157, 171, 174, 184
Monkeys: 92
Moon as spirit (wolf): 114
Moquibushito ("Old Bear"): 131, 133
Motif-Index of Folk Literature (Stith Thompson): 149
Motifs of stories: bird brings twigs to create trees for earth, 148; disorientation, 46–48, 105, 111, 121; eating or hunger as search, 26, 27, 31, 44–48, 49, 65, 68, 72, 81, 98; fish becomes a man, 177; magic hat produces warriors, 158; magic tablecloth produces food, 158; man forced to eat own flesh, 168; man speaks from fire, 168; man turns into fish, 152; meeting along a path, 2, 21, 44; mouse crawls inside anus of deer, 32, 84; mouse eats heart of deer, 32, 84; muskrat brings earth from bottom of flood, 148; raccoon crawls inside anus of deer, 32, 45, 84; raccoon eats heart of deer, 32, 45, 84; raccoon feeds dung to wolf, 45; raccoon puts dung on eyes of wolf, 46; raccoon steals food from two blind men, 125; raccoon throws bark from tree, 44–45; raccoon tricked, loses meal, 162–64; trickster covered with manure, 95; wolf bumps into trees, 46–48; wolf drowns, 48; wolf seeks river, 46–48; wolf tricked into eating dung, 45
Mouse: 32, 84, 122, 124, 182
Museums and worship: 37
Muskrat: 119, 148

Naming: 35–36
Neihardt, John: 5; see also *Black Elk Speaks*
North, James: 31–32, 79, 83–104, 135, 169, 175, 192; brother of, 93, 94, 97; grandfather of, 93, 94; grandmother of, 93, 119

Old Bear faction: 57, 93, 131
Oral history (legends): 50, 60
Oral tradition: 4, 6, 102, 184
Oster, Harry: 5, 6, 8, 11–13, 15, 17, 18, 20, 30, 33, 149
Ostracism of informants: 42
Outhouse: 11, 19, 38, 94, 101
Outsider, joking with: 36
Ownership: 20, 61

Panther: 117
Path: following, 5, 40, 104–108, 121; meeting along, 2, 21, 44; through the woods, 40, 106–108
Patience: 38, 49, 65–66, 68–69, 72, 73, 75
Perdurance: 133–34, 161, 172, 191
Powers: *see* magic powers, loss of
Powwow: 9, 17, 21, 23, 172
Presbyterian Church: 10
Promises: 21, 110, 111
Pushetonequa: 131–32

Questioning: 22, 49, 150; and fasting, 25, 49; and respect for elders, 49; and storytelling, 74, 76–77; by whites, 30, 36–37

Raccoon: 43–46, 77, 84, 124–28, 179; steals, 126, 181; both a Tokana and Kish-ko, 138; as a trickster, 162
Red Earth People: 10, 62, 112
Relatedness of all life: 13, 18–19, 113, 114, 178
Religion, Mesquakie: 16, 25, 35–36; related to language, 25
Religion, white: 113, 114
Religious freedom: 51–53, 58
Remembering: the creation, 113; "if you don't remember, you're not a Mesquakie," 111; promises, 111; stories, 22, 31
Repetition as reenactment: 74
Reservation life, Mesquakie: 7, 61
Return to Iowa from Kansas: 62
River: 44–48; see also Iowa River
Roaring in ears: 51, 107

Sacs: 10, 60, 176–78
Sacs and Foxes: 10
Sayre, Robert: 6, 8, 10, 11, 16, 31, 82
School boycott, 132; see also Mesquakie Indian Boarding School; Mesquakie Indian Day School
Secrets: 2, 41, 65, 150, 151; as gifts of spirits, 151; and past, 2; religious, 42; sharing, 151; and trust, 150
Separation of Mesquakie tribe through escape: 171
Silence: as assent, 17; awkward for non-Indian, 21, 24, 32, 50, 123, 134; as a means of communication, 67–68; as a way of saying no, 139
Singing: 16, 17, 28, 90, 96
Skinned animals: 11, 119
Skinner, Alanson: 37, 195
Skunk: 119, 182–83
Sleeping: of enemies, 171; of James Youngman, 13, 15; of wolf, 45
Snow: 68, 102, 105, 108, 135, 141, 142, 148, 175; first of winter, 72; as spirit, 114; Wisaka as snow, 148
Social division of Mesquakies: in

ceremonies and tribal games, 139; originated with Wisaka and brother, 146; see also Tokana, Kisho
Squirrels: 119
Stories: beauty of, 13, 186; belong to elders, 103; not to be changed, 54; discipline of listening to, 73, 111; meaning of, 32, 164; possible and impossible, 75; purpose of, 13; recording of, 17; religious, 16, 22, 50; sacred, 99, 144, 150; and sex, 86; as shared experiences, 160; as something that really happened, 79, 81, 153; teaching of, 13, 155, 158, 186; telling and context of, 25, 43, 72–75, 157, 158; told in winter, 157, 180
Stories, Mesquakie: "Beards and Shaving," 69–71; "Creation of Man," 111–12; "Creation of the Sacs: Coming Forth from the Water," 177–78; "Dancing Ducks," 165; "Division of the Deer into Four Parts," 117; "Dogs Named Spiro and Nixon," 36; "First Man Who Died," 143–47; "The Flood," 148; "How the Turtle Brought Ruin Upon Himself," 85–89; "Mamasa and the Escape with Bundles," 170–71; "Man with the Beard," 51–52, 110; "Man with the Magic Hat Protects Home," 160; "Man with the Magic Tablecloth and the Man with the Magic Hat," 158; "Meeting of Fox Clan with French," 112; "Mouse and the Deer," 32, 84; "One-Armed Man in Center of Island," 110; "Raccoon and the Crabs," 162–63; "Raccoon and the Ducks," 164; "Raccoon and the Wolf," 43–48, 67, 84; "Raccoons and the Deer," 32, 45, 84; Race Between the Turtle and the Deer," 75–76; "Young Man Who Fasted Overlong," 152

Stories, non-Mesquakie: "How the Raccoon Came to Live in a Tree" (Senecan), 125; "How the Racoon Tricked Two Blind Men by Stealing Their Food" (Cheyenne and many other tribes), 125; "How the Raccoon Was Told to Paint Self with Bands of Black and White" (Menomini), 127

Storyteller: can answer questions, 75; can blacken face with charcoal, 119; should be given tobacco, 73

Sturgeon, Henry: 39, 50–53, 56–60, 65–66, 68–78, 105, 110, 112, 150, 185–87

Sturgeon, Isabel: 56–60, 185–89

Sturgeon, John: 12–18, 20, 51, 70, 73, 110, 134, 176, 186–89, 191

Sturgeon, Lucy: 12, 171, 186

Sun: 24, 26, 39, 50, 135; as grandfather, 114

Swastika: 11, 93

Tama Indian Crafts Association: 27

Tape recorder: 8, 17, 20, 26, 50, 53, 135, 136, 149; reasons for reticence, 54–55

Taping of stories: 31

Tarantula: 117

Tax, Sol: 6, 13, 14, 22, 138

Telephones: Mesquakie manner on phone, 83; on settlement, 6, 83

Thunder clan: 35

Tobacco, Indian: 113, 118, 120

Tokana, 138; see also social division of Mesquakies

Trees: power of those who live in trees, 125; as spirits, 114

Trees, names of: 38, 39, 47, 48

Tribal Council, Mesquakie: 57

Tricksters: 77; see also Raccoons; motifs of stories

Turtle: 75–77, 79–81, 85–89, 101, 116, 184; and "breath of life," 89; created before man but thrown back into mud because too ugly, 101

Visions: see fasting

Wabasaiya (White Robe): 167–73, 176

Water as "source of all life": 178

Waters, John: 24–26, 102, 150

Waters, Lucille: 12, 15, 23, 34, 57, 102

Way of life, Mesquakie: 1; importance of family, 157; definition of religion, 16

Whites, coming of, 51; see also "man with beard"

"White Owl Sacred Pack": 36–37, 41

White Robe (Wabasaiya): 167–73, 176

Wickiup: 10, 12, 26, 108, 109, 115, 118, 123

Wigwam Restaurant: 9, 19, 28

Wisaka: 84, 85, 88, 99, 143–48, 154, 165; death of younger brother, 85, 89, 143–44, 154

Wolf: 43–48, 84, 114, 116, 147–48

Wolfskin, Jack: 141–49, 152, 154–66, 169–73, 188, 190–91

Wolfskin, sacred: 171

Yapata: 146, 148

Young Bear, 133; faction of, 133, 135–40, 150

Youngman, James: 12, 15, 17, 27, 29, 94

Youngman, Tom: 98–100